INDEX TO

ADMINISTRATION ACCOUNT RECORDS *OF* FREDERICK COUNTY, MARYLAND

1750-1816

L. TILDEN MOORE

HERITAGE BOOKS
2007

HERITAGE BOOKS
AN IMPRINT OF HERITAGE BOOKS, INC.

Books, CDs, and more—Worldwide

For our listing of thousands of titles see our website
at
www.HeritageBooks.com

Published 2007 by
HERITAGE BOOKS, INC.
Publishing Division
65 East Main Street
Westminster, Maryland 21157-5026

Copyright © 1996 L. Tilden Moore

Other books by the author:

1890 Special Census of the Civil War Veterans of the State of Maryland: Volume I, Garrett, Allegany and Washington Counties

Abstracts of Marriages and Deaths ... in the Newspapers of Frederick and Montgomery Counties, Maryland, 1831-1840

1890 Special Census of the Civil War Veterans of the State of Maryland: Volume II, Carroll, Frederick, Montgomery, Prince George's, Calvert, Charles and St. Mary's Counties

1890 Special Census of the Civil War Veterans of the State of Maryland: Volume III, Howard, Anne Arundel, Harford, Cecil and Kent Counties and the United States Naval Academy

1890 Special Census of the Civil War Veterans of the State of Maryland: Volume IV, Caroline, Dorchester, Queen Anne's, Somerset, Talbot, Wicomico, and Worcester

1890 Special Census of the Civil War Veterans of the State of Maryland, Volume V, Parts I and II, Baltimore City

1890 Special Census of the Civil War Veterans of the State of Maryland: Volume VII, Baltimore County and Baltimore City Institutions

All rights reserved. No part of this book may be reproduced or transmitted in any form or by any means, electronic or mechanical, including photocopying, recording or by any information storage and retrieval system without written permission from the author, except for the inclusion of brief quotations in a review.

International Standard Book Number: 978-1-8882-6585-9

FORWARD

This is just a small book in which the Register of Wills office has in its possession. It only contains 2169 names, and is an index of copies from the original Administration Account Records. These records contain valuable information that many researchers fail to check into, which will lead to other areas of research. There are 6 larger books that are available as an index to Administration account Records. Hopefully, within the next few years, these indexes will be out in book form and are dated from 1748 up to the present. The personnel of the Register of Wills office will assist you in any way they can and they welcome inquires from all over as well. For all inquires, please send a self-addressed-stamped envelop. If you think that you may have any family members that have died in Frederick County, feel free to inquire. I know that this book will be of great significant value to the genealogical community,

I wish to thank Virginia P. Fifer and her staff for all their endeavors, especially, for checking out some of the names in this book. Hopefully, within the next year, there should be a compiled index of ALL of the Wills in Frederick County, which will be a greater asset to genealogist who are researching this county. Those who are researching Frederick County may want to check into three volumes of Land records published by Patricia Abelard Andersen. These are abstracts of the early land deeds of 1748 up to 1761, so far. She has plans on continuing publishing these land records series. Forth coming, there will be several other records from the Clerk of Circuit Court Office, which will be out within the next two years.

L. Tilden Moore

VIRGINIA P. FIFER
Register

Mark A. Gelwicks
Chief Deputy

(301) 663-3722

Register of Wills
Frederick County

January, 1996

    Welcome to the Probate Records for Frederick County, Maryland. Frederick County was formed in 1748 from land designated as Prince George's County. The Index to Administration Account Records for Frederick County covers the period from 1750 to 1816. Copies of the original Accounts are located in this office, however, the originals are located in the State Archives (Hall of Records) in Annapolis. The Accounts are the financial records of the estates and contain many jewels of information for the genealogist including records as to the disposition and distribution of the assets.

                              Virginia P. Fifer
                Register of Wills for Frederick County

County Court House
100 West Patrick Street
Frederick, MD 21701-5485

	ESTATE OF		ACCOUNT	LIBER	FOLIO
1.	ALEXANDER	Elias	Account	A. #1 - (1750 - 1767)	16
2.	ARNOLD	Joseph	Account	A. #1 - (1750 - 1767)	242
3.	ANGLEBERRY	Philip	Account	A. #1 - (1750 - 1767)	263
4.	AVEY	Henry	Account	A. #1 - (1750 - 1760)	384
5.	ANDREWS	William	Account	B. #2 - (1768 - 1776)	26
6.	APLER	Everhart	Final	B. #2 - (1768 - 1776)	113
7.	AULD	Jacob	Final	B. #2 - (1768 - 1776)	218
8.	ASBESHIT	Rudy	Final	B. #2 - (1768 - 1776)	263
9.	ADAMSON	John	Final	B. #2 - (1768 - 1776)	285
10.	AVON	Archd. Revd.	Final	B. #2 - (1768 - 1776)	293
11.	ANDERSON	John	Final	B. #2 - (1768 - 1776)	343
12.	ANSTOLL	George	Account	G.M. #1 - (1777 - 1799)	64
13.	APPLE	Peter	Final	G.M. #1 - (1777 - 1799)	76
14.	ANDERS	William	Final	G.M. #1 - (1777 - 1799)	155
15.	ADAMS	Jacob	Final	G.M. #1 - (1777 - 1799)	193
16.	ALBAUGH	Zachariah	First	G.M. #1 - (1777 - 1799)	275
17.	ALBAUGH	Zachariah	Final	G.M. #1 - (1777 - 1799)	321
18.	ANDREW	Peter	Account	G.M. #1 - (1777 - 1799)	359
19.	ADAMS	Valentine	Account	G.M. #1 - (1777 - 1799)	404
20.	ADAMS	Jacob	Addl. Fl.	G.M. #1 - (1777 - 1799)	415
21.	ARNOLD	John	First	G.M. #1 - (1777 - 1799)	419
					also 450
22.	ADAMS	Valentine	Second	G.M. #1 - (1777 - 1799)	425
23.	ADAMS	Valentine	3rd & Fl.	G.M. #1 - (1777 - 1799)	447
24.	ADAMS	Christopher	Account	G.M. #1 - (1777 - 1799)	543
25.	ALBAUGH	William	Final	G.M. #1 - (1777 - 1799)	591
26.	AMBROSE	Christopher	Account	G.M. #1 - (1777 - 1799)	605
27.	ABERT	John	Final	G.M. #1 - (1777 - 1799)	629
28.	AREHART	Martin	Final	G.M. #2 - (1800 - 1805)	69
29.	ABBELON	Philip	Final	G.M. #2 - (1800 - 1805)	87
30.	ALGIER	Joseph	Final	G.M. #2 - (1800 - 1805)	100
31.	ADLESPERGER	Francis	First	G.M. #2 - (1800 - 1805)	117
32.	ALLOX	Margaret	First	G.M. #2 - (1800 - 1805)	146
33.	ALBRIGHT	John	First	G.M. #2 - (1800 - 1805)	199
34.	ADLESPERGER	Francis	Second	G.M. #2 - (1800 - 1805)	287
35.	ADAMS	Abraham	Final	G.M. #2 - (1800 - 1805)	287
36.	ADLESPERGER	Francis	Final	R.B. #1 - (1806 - 1809)	81
37.	ATER	George	Final	R.B. #1 - (1806 - 1809)	209
38.	ALLISON	John	First	R.B. #1 - (1806 - 1809)	398
39.	ALLISON	John	Second	R.B. #1 - (1806 - 1809)	405
40.	AMBROSE	Catherine	First	R.B. #1 - (1806 - 1809)	499
41.	AMBROSE	Elizabeth	Final	R.B. #2 - (1809 - 1811)	53
42.	AMBROSE	Catharine	Final	R.B. #2 - (1809 - 1811)	157
43.	ARTER	Michael	First	R.B. #2 - (1809 - 1811)	353
44.	ARTER	Michael	2nd & Fl.	R.B. #2 - (1809 - 1811)	373
45.	ARTER	Michael	2nd & Fl.	R.B. #2 - (1809 - 1811)	396
46.	ALLISON	John	Final	R.B. #2 - (1809 - 1811)	397
47.	ALBAUGH	John Senr.	First	R.B. #3 - (1812 - 1815)	22
48.	ALBAUGH	John Senr.	Second	R.B. #3 - (1812 - 1815)	83
49.	ALBAUGH	Peter	1st & Fl.	R.B. #3 - (1812 - 1815)	129
50.	ALBAUGH	John Senr.	2nd & Fl.	R.B. #3 - (1812 - 1815)	181
51.	ANGELL	Charles	First	R.B. #3 - (1812 - 1815)	259

52.	ANGELL	Charles	2nd & Fl.	R.B. #3 - (1812 - 1815)	415
53.	ANDERS	Abraham	First	H.S. #1 - (1815 - 1816)	12
54.	BRISCOE	James	Account	A. #1 - (1750 - 1767)	2
55.	BOUCKER	Peter	Account	A. #1 - (1750 - 1767)	8
56.	BURRELL	Peter	Account	A. #1 - (1750 - 1767)	13
57.	BRISCOE	James	Addl.	A. #1 - (1750 - 1767)	15
58.	BONSELL	Nicholas	Account	A. #1 - (1750 - 1767)	33
59.	BEALL	Basil	Account	A. #1 - (1750 - 1767)	103
60.	BEALL	Alexander	Addl.	A. #1 - (1750 - 1767)	119
61.	BEATTY	James	Account	A. #1 - (1750 - 1767)	120
62.	BEATTY	Edward	Account	A. #1 - (1750 - 1767)	124
63.	BEATTY	Susannah	Account	A. #1 - (1750 - 1767)	154
64.	BURGETT	Mathias	Account	A. #1 - (1750 - 1767)	201
65.	BEALL	Nathaniel	Account	A. #1 - (1750 - 1767)	207
66.	BRUCE	Williamson	Account	A. #1 - (1750 - 1767)	209
67.	BEALL	William	Account	A. #1 - (1750 - 1767)	219
68.	BEATTY	John	Account	A. #1 - (1750 - 1767)	224
69.	BEALL	Alexander	Account	A. #1 - (1750 - 1767)	227
70.	BRAWNER	Edward	Account	A. #1 - (1750 - 1767)	238
71.	BOHRER	Abraham	Account	A. #1 - (1750 - 1767)	240
72.	BEALL	Magruder Ninian	Account	A. #1 - (1750 - 1767)	252
73.	BIGGS	John	Account	A. #1 - (1750 - 1767)	273
74.	BEALL	Alexander	Addl.	A. #1 - (1750 - 1767)	275
75.	BEALL	William	Account	A. #1 - (1750 - 1767)	278
76.	BEATTY	Edward	Account	A. #1 - (1750 - 1767)	300
77.	BURTON	Eller William	Account	A. #1 - (1750 - 1767)	310
78.	BEALL	William	Addl.	A. #1 - (1750 - 1767)	315
79.	BURTON	Eller William	Addl.	A. #1 - (1750 - 1767)	320
80.	BEALL	William	2nd Addl.	A. #1 - (1750 - 1767)	324
81.	BUTLER	Peter	Account	A. #1 - (1750 - 1767)	326
82.	BEARD	John	Account	A. #1 - (1750 - 1767)	333
83.	BAKER	Nicholas	Account	A. #1 - (1750 - 1767)	334
84.	BAKER	Nicholas	Addl.	A. #1 - (1750 - 1767)	345
85.	BEAN	Wansley	Account	A. #1 - (1750 - 1767)	366
86.	BOONE	Handeal John	Account	A. #1 - (1750 - 1767)	378
87.	BLACKMARE	Charles	Account	A. #1 - (1750 - 1767)	390
88.	BEALL	Benjamin	Account	A. #1 - (1750 - 1767)	400
89.	BURTON	Eller William	2nd	A. #1 - (1750 - 1767)	416
90.	BARNES	John	Account	A. #1 - (1750 - 1767)	428
91.	BAKER	Nicholas	3rd Addl.	A. #1 - (1750 - 1767)	432
92.	BUTLER	Peter	Final	B. #2 - (1768 - 1776)	29
93.	BURTON	Eller Wm.	Final	B. #2 - (1768 - 1776)	32
94.	BROOKE	James Jr.	Final	B. #2 - (1768 - 1776)	39
95.	BOOKER	Honicle	Final	B. #2 - (1768 - 1776)	46
96.	BONTZ	Jacob	Final	B. #2 - (1768 - 1776)	59
97.	BECK	Lodowick	Final	B. #2 - (1768 - 1776)	71
98.	BACON	Thomas, Revd.	First	B. #2 - (1768 - 1776)	72
99.	BRUNNER	Jacob Jr.	Final	B. #2 - (1768 - 1776)	75
100.	BROOKE	James Junr.	Addl.	B. #2 - (1768 - 1776)	111
101.	BEALL	JosIah	Final	B. #2 - (1768 - 1776)	142
102.	BUXTON	John	Final	B. #2 - (1768 - 1776)	146
103.	BEALL	William	Final	B. #2 - (1768 - 1776)	147
104.	BOWMAN	Samuel	Final	B. #2 - (1768 - 1776)	162

105.	BURGESS	William	Final	B. #2 - (1768 - 1776)	192
106.	BAUMGARNER	Everhart	Final	B. #2 - (1768 - 1776)	198
107.	BEATTY	Susannah	Final	B. #2 - (1768 - 1776)	242
108.	BOYER	Paul	Final	B. #2 - (1768 - 1776)	248
109.	BOBRAAR	Henry	Final	B. #2 - (1768 - 1776)	272
110.	BAKER	Jacob	Final	B. #2 - (1768 - 1776)	305
111.	BRADDOCK	Henry	Final	B. #2 - (1768 - 1776)	321
112.	BRADILLER	Emanuel	Final	B. #2 - (1768 - 1776)	327
113.	BLACKAMORE	Saml.	Final	B. #2 - (1768 - 1776)	358
114.	BARRICK	Peter	Account	B. #2 - (1768 - 1776)	362
115.	BOYD	John	Account	B. #2 - (1768 - 1776)	378
116.	BRUNER	Henry	Account	G.M. #1 - (1777 - 1799)	12
117.	BARNARD	Nathaniel	Account	G.M. #1 - (1777 - 1799)	20
118.	BRUNNER	John	Account	G.M. #1 - (1777 - 1799)	30
119.	BERRYER	John	Account1	G.M. #1 - (1777 - 1799)	31
120.	BRICKER	John	Account	G.M. #1 - (1777 - 1799)	35
121.	BURNESTON	Joseph	Final	G.M. #1 - (1777 - 1799)	58
122.	BALSELL	Peter	Final	G.M. #1 - (1777 - 1799)	63
123.	BUSSARD	Samuel	Final	G.M. #1 - (1777 - 1799)	67
124.	BURY	Edward	Final	G.M. #1 - (1777 - 1799)	68
125.	BROWN	James	Final	G.M. #1 - (1777 - 1799)	73
126.	BARRICK	John	Final	G.M. #1 - (1777 - 1799)	82
127.	BUCHA	Peter	Final	G.M. #1 - (1777 - 1799)	110
128.	BOYER	Melcher	Final	G.M. #1 - (1777 - 1799)	140
129.	BRUNNER	Elias	Final	G.M. #1 - (1777 - 1799)	141
130.	BOYER	Michael	Final	G.M. #1 - (1777 - 1799)	179
131.	BRENGEL	Jacob	Final	G.M. #1 - (1777 - 1799)	188
132.	BLAIR	William	First	G.M. #1 - (1777 - 17990	194
133.	BAKER	John	Final	G.M. #1 - (1777 - 1799)	201
134.	BLAIR	William	2nd	G.M. #1 - (1777 - 1799)	209
135.	BARRICK	Christian	Final	G.M. #1 - (1777 - 1799)	222
136.	BALL	Thomas	Final	G.M. #1 - (1777 - 1799)	231
137.	BOWER	John	Final	G.M. #1 - (1777 - 1799)	254
138.	BEGGARLY	George	Final	G.M. #1 - (1777 - 1799)	258
139.	BARRICK	Handeal	Final	G.M. #1 - (1777 - 1799)	268
140.	BEAL	Elizabeth	Final	G.M. #1 - (1777 - 1799)	270
141.	BECKWITH	George	Final	G.M. #1 - (1777 - 1799)	282
142.	BROWNING	Benjamin	Final	G.M. #1 - (1777 - 1799)	286
143.	BECKWITH	George	Final	G.M. #1 - (1777 - 1799)	296
144.	BRAZETON	John	Final	G.M. #1 - (1777 - 1799)	302
145.	BEIGLER	Marks	Final	G.M. #1 - (1777 - 1799)	327
146.	BOSTIAN	Andrew	Final	G.M. #1 - (1777 - 1799)	330
147.	BAKER	William	Final	G.M. #1 - (1777 - 1799)	331
148.	BANKARD	John	Final	G.M. #1 - (1777 - 1799)	336
149.	BECKENBAUGH	Casper	Final	G.M. #1 - (1777 - 1799)	364
150.	BANKARD	Jacob	Final	G.M. #1 - (1777 - 1799)	367
151.	BEALL	Charles	Final	G.M. #1 - (1777 - 1799)	390
152.	BOARD	Jonathan	Account	G.M. #1 - (1777 - 1799)	397
153.	BROWN	Jacob	Account	G.M. #1 - (1777 - 1799)	403
154.	BUTTS	Ludwick	Final	G.M. #1 - (1777 - 1799)	409
155.	BOYER	Henry	Account	G.M. #1 - (1777 - 1799)	412
156.	BECKENBAUGH	Casper			441
157.	BLACK	Andrew	First	G.M. #1 - (1777 - 1799)	446

#	Surname	Given Name	Type	Reference	Page
158.	BEALL	Charles	Addl. Fl.	G.M. #1 - (1777 - 1799)	449
159.	BURKETT	Nathaniel	Final	G.M. #1 - (1777 - 1799)	466
160.	BLACK	Andrew	Final	G.M. #1 - (1777 - 1799)	475
161.	BANDER	Sebold	Final	G.M. #1 - (1777 - 1799)	476
162.	BLAIR	William	Third	G.M. #1 - (1777 - 1799)	485
163.	BARRICK	William	Account	G.M. #1 - (1777 - 1799)	487
164.	BECKENBAUGH	Casper	Final	G.M. #1 - (1777 - 1799)	488
165.	BEARD	Jonathan	Second	G.M. #1 - (1777 - 1799)	495
166.	BOMGART	Ludwick	Account	G.M. #1 - (1777 - 1799)	496
167.	BOYER	Casper	Account	G.M. #1 - (1777 - 1799)	510
168.	BITESELL	Henry	Account	G.M. #1 - (1777 - 1799)	515
169.	BITESELL	Henry	Final	G.M. #1 - (1777 - 1799)	518
170.	BLACKBURN	John	Account	G.M. #1 - (1777 - 1799)	525
171.	BECKER	Christian	Account	G.M. #1 - (1777 - 1799)	527
172.	BEALL	James	Account	G.M. #1 - (1777 - 1799)	533
173.	BRADNECK	Henry	Account	G.M. #1 - (1777 - 1799)	566
174.	BOOKER	Bartholomew	Account	G.M. #1 - (1777 - 1799)	594
175.	BENSER	Godlip	Account	G.M. #1 - (1777 - 1799)	602
176.	BROADBECK	Mathias	Account	G.M. #1 - (1777 - 1799)	624
177.	BOOKEY	Mathias	Account	G.M. #1 - (1777 - 1799)	628
178.	BEATTY	Thomas	Account	G.M. #1 - (1777 - 1799)	637
179.	BRAYFIELD	Jane	Account	G.M. #1 - (1777 - 1799)	652
180.	BONTLEY	Abner	Account	G.M. #1 - (1777 - 1799)	662
181.	BEARD	Jonathan	Final	G.M. #2 - (1800 - 1805)	1
182.	BRANGLE	Christian	Final	G.M. #2 - (1800 - 1805)	15
183.	BURRIER	Leonard	Account	G.M. #2 - (1800 - 1805)	64
184.	BURRIER	Leonard	Final	G.M. #2 - (1800 - 1805)	80
185.	BROTHER	Henry	Final	G.M. #2 - (1800 - 1805)	133
186.	BECKENBAUGH	George	First	G.M. #2 - (1800 - 1805)	136
187.	BRENGLE	Lawrence	Final	G.M. #2 - (1800 - 1805)	168
188.	BECKENBAUGH	George	2nd	G.M. #2 - (1800 - 1805)	237
189.	BLACK	Joseph	First	G.M. #2 - (1800 - 1805)	246
190.	BROWN	Daniel	Final	G.M. #2 - (1800 - 1805)	277
191.	BLACK	Joseph	2nd	G.M. #2 - (1800 - 1805)	283
192.	BOWER	Christian	Final	G.M. #2 - (1800 - 1805)	285
193.	BLACK	Andrew	Final	G.M. #2 - (1800 - 1805)	298
194.	BURRIER	Philip	Final	G.M. #2 - (1800 - 1805)	306
195.	BOYER	Hubartus	Final	G.M. #2 - (1800 - 1805)	315
196.	BEAN	James	First	G.M. #2 - (1800 - 1805)	321
197.	BLACK	Joseph	Final	G.M. #2 - (1800 - 1805)	323
198.	BEARD	Peter	First	G.M. #2 - (1800 - 1805)	348
199.	BEAN	James	Second	G.M. #2 - (1800 - 1805)	353
200.	BEALL	Joseph	Final	G.M. #2 - (1800 - 1805)	370
201.	BEATTY	William	First	G.M. #2 - (1800 - 1805)	443
202.	BALTZELL	Daniel	First	G.M. #2 - (1800 - 1805)	451
203.	BOYER	Casper	Final	G.M. #2 - (1800 - 1805)	454
204.	BEARD	Peter	Final	G.M. #2 - (1800 - 1805)	457
205.	BOST	Michael	Final	R.B. #1 - (1806 - 1809)	102
206.	BOWLUS	Nicholas	Final	R.B. #1 - (1806 - 1809)	122
207.	BEALL	Ann	Final	R.B. #1 - (1806 - 1809)	162
208.	BROWER	Jacob	Final	R.B. #1 - (1806 - 1809)	200
209.	BUCKEY	John	Final	R.B. #1 - (1806 - 1809)	213
210.	BELL	Peter	1st & Fl.	R.B. #1 - (1806 - 1809)	220

211.	BROADBECK	Henry	Final	R.B. #1 - (1806 - 1809)	222
212.	BABILON	Barbara	Final	R.B. #1 - (1806 - 1809)	231
213.	BOYER	Charlotte	Final	R.B. #1 - (1806 - 1809)	237
214.	BRYAN	David	First	R.B. #1 - (1806 - 1809)	247
215.	BURCKHART	George	First	R.B. #1 - (1806 - 1809)	329
216.	BOYER	Philip	Final	R.B. #1 - (1806 - 1809)	335
217.	BOTTENBERG	Michael	Final	R.B. #1 - (1806 - 1809)	391
218.	BAER	George Sr.	Final	R.B. #1 - (1806 - 1809)	430
219.	BRAYFIELD	Samuel	Final	R.B. #1 - (1806 - 1809)	436
220.	BAKER	Frederick	Final	R.B. #1 - (1806 - 1809)	478
221.	BEALL	Rachel	Final	R.B. #2 - (1809 - 1811)	2
222.	BEATTY	William	Second	R.B. #2 - (1809 - 1811)	50
223.	BLACK	Joseph	2nd & Fl.	R.B. #2 - (1809 - 1811)	77
224.	BOYER	Catherine	First	R.B. #2 - (1809 - 1811)	79
225.	BECKENBAUGH	George	Third	R.B. #2 - (1809 - 1811	121
226.	BUZARD	Jacob	Final	R.B. #2 - (1809 - 1811)	134
227.	BALTZELL	Jacob	First	R.B. #2 - (1809 - 1811)	142
228.	BONHM	Malachia	1st & Fl.	R.B. #2 - (1809 - 1811)	150
229.	BUTTS	Christian	First	R.B. #2 - (1809 - 1811)	154
230.	BOUGHER	Jacob	First	R.B. #2 - (1809 - 1811)	179
231.	BEATTY	William	Final	R.B. #2 - (1809 - 1811)	187
232.	BLACK	Catharine	First	R.B. #2 - (1809 - 1811)	189
233.	BOST	Valentine	Final	R.B. #2 - (1809 - 1811)	191
234.	BLACK	Catharine	Final	R.B. #2 - (1809 - 1811)	248
235.	BELLWOOD	Henry	First	R.B. #2 - (1809 - 1811)	266
236.	BROWN	Henry Sr.	First	R.B. #2 - (1809 - 1811)	268
237.	BURKHART	George	Second	R.B. #2 - (1809 - 1811)	286
238.	BOND	Edward	First	R.B. #2 - (1809 - 1811)	298
239.	BALTZELL	Daniel	Final	R.B. #2 - (1809 - 1811)	323
240.	BOND	Edward	Final	R.B. #2 - (1809 - 1811)	327
241.	BALTZELL	Jacob	Final	R.B. #2 - (1809 - 1811)	339
242.	BUCKEY	Mathias	Final	R.B. #2 - (1809 - 1811)	351
243.	BEAN	James	Third	R.B. #2 - (1809 - 1811)	360
244.	BEALL	Charles	2nd Addl.	R.B. #2 - (1809 - 1811)	411
245.	BUTTS	John	First	R.B. #2 - (1809 - 1811)	413
246.	BUTTMAN	Mary	1st & Fl.	R.B. #2 - (1809 - 1811)	468
247.	BEAN	James	Fourth	R.B. #2 - (1809 - 1811)	480
248.	BEEL	David	1st & Fl.	R.B. #2 - (1809 - 1811)	489
249.	BEGHT	Jacob Jr.	First	R.B. #3 - (1812 - 1815)	20
250.	BOWERS	Stephen	Final	R.B. #3 - (1812 - 1815)	25
251.	BURKHART	George	3rd & Fl.	R.B. #3 - (1812 - 1815)	68
252.	BEGHT	Jacob Jr.	2nd & FL.	R.B. #3 - (1812 - 1815)	91
253.	BEATTY	Dorothy Mary	First	R.B. #3 - (1812 - 1815)	93
254.	BOYERLY	Jacob	1st & Fl.	R.B. #3 - (1812 - 1815)	95
255.	BELLWOOD	Joseph	First	R.B. #3 - (1812 - 1815)	116
256.	BALDWIN	Elijah	Final	R.B. #3 - (1812 - 1815)	119
257.	BELLWOOD	Henry	Final	R.B. #3 - (1812 - 1815)	130
258.	BROWN	Christopher	First	R.B. #3 - (1812 - 1815)	154
259.	BROWN	George	First	R.B. #3 - (1812 - 1815)	271
260.	BURN	Henry	First	R.B. #3 - (1812 - 1815)	318
261.	BUSSARD	Daniel	1st & Fl	R.B. #3 - (1812 - 1815)	346
262.	BROWN	George	2nd & Fl.	R.B. #3 - (1812 - 1815)	354
263.	BLESSING	Jacob	1st & Fl.	R.B. #3 - (1812 - 1815)	420

#	Surname	Given	Type	Book	Page
264.	BISHOP	John	1st & Fl.	R.B. #3 - (1812 - 1815)	422
265.	BURKHART	John	First	R.B. #3 - (1812 - 1815)	435
266.	BRENGLE	George	1st & Fl.	H.S. #1 - (1815 - 1816)	9
267.	BOOSE	Peter	1st & Fl.	H.S. #1 - (1815 - 1816)	10
268.	BRADLEY	William	First	H.S. #1 - (1815 - 1816)	21
269.	BURKHART	John	2nd & Fl.	H.S. #1 - (1815 - 1816)	36
270.	BOUGHER	Jacob	2nd & Fl.	H.S. #1 - (1815 - 1816)	56
271.	BOWERS	John	1st & Fl.	H.S. #1 - (1815 - 1816)	142
272.	COOMBS	Richard	Account	A. #1 - (1750 - 1767)	22
273.	CARROLL	Daniel	Account	A. #1 - (1750 - 1767)	60
274.	COOPER	William	Account	A. #1 - (1750 - 1767)	211
275.	CONN	Thomas	Account	A. #1 - (1750 - 1767)	214
276.	COLP	Nicholas	Account	A. #1 - (1750 - 1767)	215
277.	CHEESE	Jacob George	Account	A. #1 - (1750 - 1767)	218
278.	CONN	Thomas	Addl.	A. #1 - (1750 - 1767)	257
279.	CLARKE	George	Account	A. #1 - (1750 - 1767)	266
280.	CONN	Thomas	2nd Addl.	A. #1 - (1750 - 1767)	292
281.	CONN	Thomas	3rd Addl.	A. #1 - (1750 - 1767)	329
282.	CHAPLINE	Moses	Account	A. #1 - (1750 - 1767)	374
283.	CHAPLINE	Moses	2nd	A. #1 - (1750 - 1767)	414
284.	CAMPBELL	Hugh	Account	A. #1 - (1750 - 1767)	430
285.	CROUSE	Jacob	Account	A. #1 - (1750 - 1767)	445
286.	CROUSE	Jacob	Final	B. #2 - (1768 - 1776)	119
287.	CREAGER	Casper	Final	B. #2 - (1768 - 1776)	126
288.	CREAGAR	Christian	Final	B. #2 - (1768 - 1776)	128
289.	CROUSE	Jacob	Final	B. #2 - (1768 - 1776)	155
290.	CARNHART	Henry	Final	B. #2 - (1768 - 1776)	165
291.	CRAMER	Jacob	Final	B. #2 - (1768 - 1776)	167
292.	CHANEY	Ezekiel	Final	B. #2 - (1768 - 1776)	205
293.	CLARK	Joseph	Final	B. #2 - (1768 - 1776)	209
294.	COPER	Mary Ann	Final	B. #2 - (1768 - 1776)	217
295.	COONCE	Nicholas	Final	B. #2 - (1768 - 1776)	262
296.	CORNALL	Smith	Final	B. #2 - (1768 - 1776)	280
297.	CARRICK	James	Account	B. #2 - (1768 - 1776)	300
298.	CASE	Simeon	Final	B. #2 - (1768 - 1776)	307
299.	CLEM	George	Final	B. #2 - (1768 - 1776)	314
300.	COOK	John	Account	B. #2 - (1768 - 1776)	329
301.	CROUS	Vendal	Final	B. #2 - (1768 - 1776)	344
302.	CHANEY	Richard	Final	B. #2 - (1768 - 1776)	349
303.	CARMACK	William	Account	G.M. #1 - (1777 - 1799)	28
304.	CARNUFF	Henry	Account	G.M. #1 - (1777 - 1799)	40
305.	COFFEE	Philip	Final	G.M. #1 - (1777 - 1799)	90
306.	COILER	George	Final	G.M. #1 - (1777 - 1799)	91
307.	COONCE	Peter	First	G.M. #1 - (1777 - 1799)	101
308.	CROUCH	James	Final	G.M. #1 - (1777 - 1799)	119
309.	CLABOUGH	Frederick	First	G.M. #1 - (1777 - 1799)	134
310.	CASSOLL	John	First	G.M. #1 - (1777 - 1799)	169
311.	CRAWL	Christian	Final	G.M. #1 - (1777 - 1799)	188
312.	CRAWL	Henry	First	G.M. #1 - (1777 - 1799)	205
313.	CROWL	Henry	Final	G.M. #1 - (1777 - 1799)	223
314.	CREAGER	Michael	Final	G.M. #1 - (1777 - 1799)	228
315.	CREPPS	Jacob	First	G.M. #1 - (1777 - 1799)	231
316.	CRUMBECKER	Jacob	Final	G.M. #1 - (1777 - 1799)	245

317.	COLLINS	Jacob	Account	G.M. #1 - (1777 - 1799)	291
318.	COONCE	Peter	Final	G.M. #1 - (1777 - 1799)	310
319.	CARTER	John	Final	G.M. #1 - (1777 - 1799)	317
320.	CRAWMER	George	Final	G.M. #1 - (1777 - 1799)	320
321.	CAMMELL	Leonard	Account	G.M. #1 - (1777 - 1799)	322
322.	CRUM	Martha	Final	G.M. #1 - (1777 - 1799)	328
323.	CROMWELL	Joseph	Final	G.M. #1 - (1777 - 1799)	332
324.	CRIDER	Barbara	Account	G.M. #1 - (1777 - 1799)	341
325.	CALEPAUGH	Francis	Final	G.M. #1 - (1777 - 1799)	350
326.	CLEM	George	Account	G.M. #1 - (1777 - 1799)	362
327.	CYFERT	Henry	Final	G.M. #1 - (1777 - 1799)	376
328.	CROMMETT	Jacob	Final	G.M. #1 - (1777 - 1799)	382
329.	CRAWMER	George	Final	G.M. #1 - (1777 - 1799)	432
330.	CLAY	George	Final	G.M. #1 - (1777 - 1799)	443
331.	CRUM	William	Account	G.M. #1 - (1777 - 1799)	454
332.	CROSS	Henry	Final	G.M. #1 - (1777 - 1799)	478
333.	COPLIN	James	Account	G.M. #1 - (1777 - 1799)	508
334.	CRIST	Jacob	Account	G.M. #1 - (1777 - 1799)	554
335.	CAMPBELL	James	Account	G.M. #1 - (1777 - 1799)	557
336.	CURRANS	William	Account	G.M. #1 - (1777 - 1799)	579
337.	CHISHOLME	John	Account	G.M. #1 - (1777 - 1799)	599
338.	COLEMAN	Cornelius	Account	G.M. #1 - (1777 - 1799)	601
339.	CAMPBELL	Leonard	Addl. Fl.	G.M. #1 - (1777 - 1799)	606
340.	CRUISE	Paul	Account	G.M. #1 - (1777 - 1799)	613
341.	CRUISE	Paul	Addl. Fl.	G.M. #1 - (1777 - 1799)	621
342.	CUMMING	William	Account	G.M. #1 - (1777 - 1799)	623
343.	CARVER	Samuel	Final	G.M. #1 - (1777 - 1799)	630
344.	CARVER	Samuel	Final	G.M. #1 - (1777 - 1799)	631
345.	CRIST	Jacob	Final	G.M. #1 - (1777 - 1799)	638
346.	CRISER	Adam	Account	G.M. #1 - (1777 - 1799)	639
347.	COLLINS	Humphrey	Final	G.M. #1 - (1777 - 1799)	660
348.	CRAMER	George	Final	G.M. #1 - (1777 - 1799)	668
349.	COONTZ	William	Final	G.M. #2 - (1800 - 1805)	45
350.	CAIN	William	Final	G.M. #2 - (1800 - 1805)	48
351.	CRAPSTER	Ruliff	Final	G.M. #2 - (1800 - 1805)	55
352.	CRUISE	Paul	2nd Addl.	G.M. #2 - (1800 - 1805)	88
353.	CLABAUGH	Samuel	Account	G.M. #2 - (1800 - 1805)	91
354.	CROUSE	John	Final	G.M. #2 - (1800 - 1805)	94
355.	CAIN	John	Final	G.M. #2 - (1800 - 1805)	101
356.	CHARLTON	Eleanor	Account	G.M. #2 - (1800 - 1805)	107
357.	COMP	Peter	Final	G.M. #2 - (1800 - 1805)	121
358.	CHARLTON	Eleanor	Final	G.M. #2 - (1800 - 1805)	135
359.	CARR	Thomas	First	G.M. #2 - (1800 - 1805)	233
360.	CHONOEWTH	Thomas	First	G.M. #2 - (1800 - 1805)	256
361.	CARMACK	John	Final	G.M. #2 - (1800 - 1805)	282
362.	CARR	Thomas	2nd	G.M. #2 - (1800 - 1805)	292
363.	CLABAUGH	Samuel	Final	G.M. #2 - (1800 - 1805)	378
364.	CRAMER	Adam	First	G.M. #2 - (1800 - 1805)	395
365.	CRAMER	Casper	Final	G.M. #2 - (1800 - 1805)	397
000.	CARR	Thomas	Final	G.M. #2 - (1800 - 1805)	398
367.	CRAMER	Adam	2nd	G.M. #2 - (1800 - 1805)	411
368.	CHANEY	William	1st	G.M. #2 - (1800 - 1805)	421
369.	CLOSE	George	Final	G.M. #2 - (1800 - 1805)	432

370.	CRAMER	Adam	Final	G.M. #2 - (1800 - 1805)	458
371.	CHANEY	William	2nd	G.M. #2 - (1800 - 1805)	474
372.	CRONICE	John	Final	G.M. #2 - (1800 - 1805)	490
373.	CHANEY	William	Third	G.M. #3 - (1806 - 1809)	1
374.	CARN	John	Final	R.B. #3 - (1806 - 1809)	33
375.	COLEGATE	John	First	R.B. #3 - (1806 - 1809)	36
376.	CORNELL	Benjamin	First	R.B. #3 - (1806 - 1809)	38
377.	CARBERY	B. John	First	R.B. #3 - (1806 - 1809)	41
378.	CRUMBAUGH	David	Final	R.B. #3 - (1806 - 1809)	61
379.	CUBLENTZ	Philip	Final	R.B. #3 - (1806 - 1809)	68
380.	CRAFT	Frederick Jr.	Final	R.B. #3 - (1806 - 1809)	100
381.	CHANEY	William	Fourth	R.B. #3 - (1806 - 1809)	104
382.	CARTY	Thomas	First	R.B. #1 - (1806 - 1809)	116
383.	CARTY	Thomas	Final	R.B. #1 - (1806 - 1809)	129
384.	CURFFMAN	Daniel	First	R.B. #1 - (1806 - 1809)	153
385.	CRETIN	James	First	R.B. #1 - (1806 - 1809)	166
386.	CAIN	Ann	Final	R.B. #1 - (1806 - 1809)	249
387.	CORNALL	Benjamin	Second	R.B. #1 - (1806 - 1809)	337
388.	CHANEY	William	Fifth	R.B. #1 - (1806 - 1809)	342
389.	COLEGATE	John	2nd	R.B. #1 - (1806 - 1809)	363
390.	COLEGATE	John	3rd	R.B. #1 - (1806 - 1809)	376
391.	CASTLE	Thomas	Final	R.B. #1 - (1806 - 1809)	379
392.	CHENOWETH	Thomas	Final	R.B. #1 - (1806 - 1809)	383
393.	CRAMER	William	First	R.B. #1 - (1806 - 1809)	428
394.	CRISE	Joseph	First	R.B. #1 - (1806 - 1809)	420
395.	CRUMBAUGH	Conrad	Final	R.B. #1 - (1806 - 1809)	440
396.	CRISE	Joseph	2nd	R.B. #1 - (1806 - 1809)	454
397.	COLEGATE	John	Final	R.B. #1 - (1806 - 1809)	468
398.	CRYSLER	Peter	Final	R.B. #1 - (1806 - 1809)	482
399.	CHARLTON	John Usher	1st & Fl.	R.B. #1 - (1806 - 1809)	487
400.	CRAIG	John	1st & Fl.	R.B. #1 - (1806 - 1809)	497
401.	CUMMIN	James	First	R.B. #2 - (1809 - 1811)	59
402.	CHANEY	William	Sixth	R.B. #2 - (1809 - 1811)	65
403.	CHANEY	William	Seventh	R.B. #2 - (1809 - 1811)	66
404.	CHANEY	William	Final	R.B. #2 - (1809 - 1811)	75
405.	CRONE	Conrad	Final	R.B. #2 - (1809 - 1811)	76
406.	CLAREY	William	Final	R.B. #2 - (1809 - 1811)	87
407.	CRAMER	William	Final	R.B. #2 - (1809 - 1811)	94
408.	CREAGER	Conrad	Final	R.B. #2 - (1809 - 1811)	109
409.	COOMES	Baalis	First	R.B. #2 - (1809 - 1811)	144
410.	CURFMAN	Daniel Jr.	First	R.B. #2 - (1809 - 1811)	168
411.	CRISE	Joseph	Final	R.B. #2 - (1809 - 1811)	270
412.	COOMES	Baalis	2nd	R.B. #2 - (1809 - 1811)	313
413.	CLARY	Benjamin Jr.	Final	R.B. #2 - (1809 - 1811)	349
414.	COOMES	Baalis	Third	R.B. #2 - (1809 - 1811)	375
415.	CURFMAN	Daniel	2nd	R.B. #2 - (1809 - 1811)	394
416.	CURFMAN	Daniel	3rd	R.B. #2 - (1809 - 1811)	398
417.	COOMES	Baalis	Final	R.B. #2 - (1809 - 1811)	414
418.	CRETIN	James	2nd & Fl.	R.B. #2 - (1809 - 1811)	419
419.	CRUM	William Sr.	First	R.B. #2 - (1809 - 1811)	475
420.	CRUM	William Sr.	2nd & Fl.	R.B. #2 - (1809 - 1811)	496
421.	CREATON	Elizabeth	1st & Fl.	R.B. #3 - (1812 - 1815)	1
422.	CREAGER	Adam	First	R.B. #3 - (1812 - 1815)	4

423.	CRAMER	Peter	1st & Fl.	R.B. #3 - (1812 - 1815)	46
424.	CRISE	John	1st & Fl.	R.B. #3 - (1812 - 1815)	112
425.	CUMMING	William	Final	R.B. #3 - (1812 - 1815)	208
426.	COVER	Earhart	First	R.B. #3 - (1812 - 1815)	234
427.	COOPER	James	First	R.B. #3 - (1812 - 1815)	241
428.	COVER	Earhart	2nd & Fl.	R.B. #3 - (1812 - 1815)	267
429.	COOPER	Robert	First	R.B. #3 - (1812 - 1815)	370
430.	CRAPSTER	Abraham	1st & Fl.	R.B. #3 - (1812 - 1815)	386
431.	COOPER	Robert	Second	R.B. #3 - (1812 - 1815)	413
432.	COOPER	James	1st	R.B. #3 - (1812 - 1815)	414
433.	COOPER	James	Second	R.B. #3 - (1812 - 1815)	418
434.	CARN	Magdalena	1st & Fl.	H.S. #1 - (1815 - 1816)	27
435.	COOKES	Jacob	First	H.S. #1 - (1815 - 1816)	34
436.	COOLEY	James	First	H.S. #1 - (1815 - 1816)	64
437.	COOLEY	James	2nd	H.S. #1 - (1815 - 1816)	64
438.	CURFMAN	Daniel	4th	H.S. #1 - (1815 - 1816)	85
439.	CRONISE	Henry Sr.	1st & Fl.	H.S. #1 - (1815 - 1816)	89
440.	CRUM	Amelia	1st & Fl.	H.S. #1 - (1815 - 1816)	249
441.	DAVIS	John	Account	A. #1 - (1760 - 1767)	12
442.	DAVIS	Meredith	Account	A. #1 - (1760 - 1767)	35
443.	DAVIS	Meredith	Addl.	A. #1 - (1760 - 1767)	46
444.	DAVIS	Thomas	Account	A. #1 - (1760 - 1767)	49
445.	DURBIN	Samuel	Account	A. #1 - (1760 - 1767)	52
446.	DAVIS	Meredith	Addl.	A. #1 - (1760 - 1767)	141
447.	DEVILBISS	Michael	Account	A. #1 - (1760 - 1767)	152
448.	DEVILBISS	Michael	Addl.	A. #1 - (1760 - 1767)	156
449.	DUNN	Margarett	Account	A. #1 - (1760 - 1767)	157
450.	DEBUTTS	Robert	Account	A. #1 - (1760 - 1767)	161
451.	DOWNEY	Robert	Account	A. #1 - (1760 - 1767)	212
452.	DOWDEN	Michael	Account	A. #1 - (1760 - 1767)	248
453.	DAVIS	Daniel	Account	A. #1 - (1760 - 1767)	317
454.	DUCKETT	Jacob	Account	A. #1 - (1760 - 1767)	358
455.	DAVIS	Daniel	Addl.	A. #1 - (1760 - 1767)	364
456.	DAVIS	Daniel	3rd Addl.	A. #1 - (1760 - 1767)	426
457.	DELAUDER	David	Account	B. #2 - (1768 - 1776)	7
458.	DICKSON	James	Account	B. #2 - (1768 - 1776)	13
459.	DAVIS	Ann	Account	B. #2 - (1768 - 1776)	19
460.	DOUGLASS	Robert	Account	B. #2 - (1768 - 1776)	35
461.	DYAL	William	Final	B. #2 - (1768 - 1776)	98
462.	DUCKER	William	Account	B. #2 - (1768 - 1776)	103
463.	DUCKER	William	Final	B. #2 - (1768 - 1776)	154
464.	DAVIS	Meredith	Final	B. #2 - (1768 - 1776)	160
465.	DANNER, (see TANNER, Peter)				170
466.	DAVIS	Cornelius	Account	B. #2 - (1768 - 1776)	194
467.	DAVIS	Vachel	Account	B. #2 - (1768 - 1776)	333
468.	DAVIS	Benjamin	Final	B. #2 - (1768 - 1776)	351
469.	DAVIS	Vachel	Final	B. #2 - (1768 - 1776)	370
470.	DEVILBISS	Casper	Account	G.M. #1 - (1777 - 1799)	21
471.	DAVIS	Enoch	Account	G.M. #1 - (1777 - 1799)	83
472.	DELASHMUTT	Elias	Final	G.M. #1 - (1777 - 1799)	86
473.	DENVER	William	Final	G.M. #1 - (1777 - 1799)	163
474.	DEVILBISS	George	First	G.M. #1 - (1777 - 1799)	212
475.	DEVILBISS	George	Final	G.M. #1 - (1777 - 1799)	222

476.	DILL	Nicholas	Fianl	G.M. #1 - (1777 - 1799)	225
477.	DORSEY	Crockett	First	G.M. #1 - (1777 - 1799)	242
478.	DEHOFF	Philip	Final	G.M. #1 - (1777 - 1799)	315
479.	DORSEY	John C.	Second	G.M. #1 - (1777 - 1799)	366
480.	DEVENBOUGH	Christopher	Final	G.M. #1 - (1777 - 1799)	409
481.	DORSEY	J. Crockett	Third	G.M. #1 - (1777 - 1799)	411
482.	DYER	Edward	Account	G.M. #1 - (1777 - 1799)	423
483.	DEVILBISS	Adam	Account	G.M. #1 - (1777 - 1799)	517
484.	DELASHMUTT	Lindsey	Account	G.M. #1 - (1777 - 1799)	552
485.	DORSEY	William	Account	G.M. #1 - (1777 - 1799)	570
486.	DOWNWOLF	Ann M.	Account	G.M. #1 - (1777 - 1799)	609
487.	DAVIS	Richard	Account	G.M. #1 - (1777 - 1799)	614
488.	DEAN	John	Account	G.M. #1 - (1777 - 1799)	664
489.	DORSEY	William	Second	G.M. #2 - (1800 - 1805)	1
490.	DEAN	John	Final	G.M. #2 - (1800 - 1805)	4
491.	DERN	Isaac	Final	G.M. #2 - (1800 - 1805)	34
492.	DORSEY	A. David	Final	G.M. #2 - (1800 - 1805)	81
493.	DERR	Michael Geo.	Final	G.M. #2 - (1800 - 1805)	99
494.	DELASHMUTT	Lindsey	Final	G.M. #2 - (1800 - 1805)	177
495.	DURST	Henry	Final	G.M. #2 - (1800 - 1805)	337
496.	DERR	Sebastian	Final	G.M. #2 - (1800 - 1805)	339
497.	DORSEY	William	Final	G.M. #2 - (1800 - 1805)	449
498.	DEVILBISS	John	Final	G.M. #2 - (1800 - 1805)	486
499.	DAVIS	Richard	Final	G.M. #2 - (1800 - 1805)	488
500.	DERN	Frederick	First	R.B. #1 - (1806 - 1809)	22
501.	DERN	Frederick	Final	R.B. #1 - (1806 - 1809)	28
502.	DEVILBISS	Geo. Sr.	First	R.B. #1 - (1806 - 1809)	31
503.	DEHOOF	John	Final	R.B. #1 - (1806 - 1809)	63
504.	DEVILBISS	Geo. Jr.	First	R.B. #1 - (1806 - 1809)	98
505.	DEBELLEVUE	St. M. Charles	Account	R.B. #1 - (1806 - 1809)	182
506.	DEAN	Hezekiah	First	R.B. #1 - (1806 - 1809)	204
507.	DORNER	Andrew	First	R.B. #1 - (1806 - 1809)	295
508.	DOFLER	Peter	1st & Fl.	R.B. #1 - (1806 - 1809)	299
509.	DINTERMAN	Henry	Final	R.B. #1 - (1806 - 1809)	311
510.	DOLL	Joseph Jr.	Final	R.B. #1 - (1806 - 1809)	321
511.	DAVIS	Walter	Final	R.B. #1 - (1806 - 1809)	332
512.	DAVIS	Luke	Final	R.B. #1 - (1806 - 1809)	348
513.	DEVILBISS	George Sr.	Second	R.B. #1 - (1806 - 1809)	363
514.	DAVIS	Elias	First	R.B. #1 - (1806 - 1809)	369
515.	DERNER	Andrew	Final	R.B. #1 - (1806 - 1809)	377
516.	DERN	William	First	R.B. #1 - (1806 - 1809)	408
517.	DELAWTER	Jacob	First	R.B. #1 - (1806 - 1809)	426
518.	DEVILBISS	George Jr.	Second	R.B. #1 - (1806 - 1809)	451
519.	DERN	William	Second	R.B. #2 - (1809 - 1811)	42
520.	DERN	William	Third	R.B. #2 - (1809 - 1811)	44
521.	DOLL	George	Final	R.B. #2 - (1809 - 1811)	81
522.	DUDDERER	Jacob	Final	R.B. #2 - (1809 - 1811)	105
523.	DELAWTER	Jacob	Second	R.B. #2 - (1809 - 1811)	108
524.	DAWSON	Nicholas	First	R.B. #2 - (1809 - 1811)	159
525.	DAVIS	Elias	Final	R.B. #2 - (1809 - 1811)	170
526.	DEVILBISS	Christian	Final	R.B. #2 - (1809 - 1811)	252
527.	DERNER	Jacob	Final	R.B. #2 - (1809 - 1811)	254
528.	DORSEY	Joshua Edw.	First	R.B. #2 - (1809 - 1811)	290

529.	DORSEY	Joshua Edw.	Final	R.B. #2 - (1809 - 1811)	301
530.	DERN	William	Fourth	R.B. #2 - (1809 - 1811)	378
531.	DAMAN	Frederick	1st & Fl.	R.B. #2 - (1809 - 1811)	470
532.	DELASHMUTT	Trammell	First	R.B. #3 - (1812 - 1815)	10
533.	DEVILBISS	George Sr.	First	R.B. #3 - (1812 - 1815)	139
534.	DUVALL	Samuel	1st & Fl.	R.B. #3 - (1812 - 1815)	187
535.	DERR	Martin John	1st & Fl.	R.B. #3 - (1812 - 1815)	205
536.	DIFFENDAL	John	1st & Fl.	R.B. #3 - (1812 - 1815)	229
537.	DAVIS	Mary	First	R.B. #3 - (1812 - 1815)	249
538.	DAVIS	Mary	2nd & Fl.	R.B. #3 - (1812 - 1815)	256
539.	DAVIS	Amos Jr.	1st & Fl.	R.B. #3 - (1812 - 1815)	276
540.	DELASHMUTT	Trammell	Second	R.B. #3 - (1812 - 1815)	294
541.	DOUB	George	1st & Fl.	R.B. #3 - (1812 - 1815)	341
542.	DEVILBISS	John H.	First	H.S. #1 - (1815 - 1816)	82
543.	DARNALL	Thomas	1st & Fl.	H.S. #1 - (1815 - 1816)	103
544.	DARNALL	Rachel	1st & Fl.	H.S. #1 - (1815 - 1816)	126
545.	DARNALL	John	First	H.S. #1 - (1815 - 1816)	131
546.	DARNALL	William	First	H.S. #1 - (1815 - 1816)	133
547.	DUTTEROW	Conrad of Jacob	First	H.S. #1 - (1815 - 1816)	160
548.	DEMMITT	Henry	1st & Fl.	H.S. #1 - (1815 - 1816)	178
549.	DEVILBISS	John	Final	H.S. #1 - (1815 - 1816)	210
550.	DARNALL	William	2nd & Fl.	H.S. #1 - (1815 - 1816)	214
551.	DELAWTER	Jacob	3rd & Fl.	H.S. #1 - (1815 - 1816)	217
552.	DELASHMUTT	Trammel	Third	H.S. #1 - (1815 - 1816)	237
553.	DARNALL	John	Second	H.S. #1 - (1815 - 1816)	241
554.	DEVILBISS	Margaret	1st & Fl.	H.S. #1 - (1815 - 1816)	243
555.	ELTINGE	Cornelius	Account	A. #1 - (1750 - 1767)	70
556.	ELTINGE	Rudolph	Account	A. #1 - (1750 - 1767)	230
557.	ELTINGE	Rudolph	Account	A. #1 - (1750 - 1767)	352
558.	ELTINGE	Rudolph	Account	A. #1 - (1750 - 1767)	359
559.	EVERHART	Christopher	Account	A. #1 - (1750 - 1767)	397
560.	EVERHART	Andrew	Final	B. #2 - (1768 - 1776)	136
561.	EVANS	Robert	Final	B. #2 - (1768 - 1776)	169
562.	EASON	John	Final	B. #2 - (1768 - 1776)	296
563.	ECKMAN	Jacob	Account	G.M. #1 - (1777 - 1799)	23
564.	ERB	Peter	Account	G.M. #1 - (1776 - 1799)	34
565.	ELLER	Geo. Michael	Final	G.M. #1 - (1776 - 1799)	61
566.	EVANS	John	First	G.M. #1 - (1776 - 1799)	88
567.	EADER	Casper	Final	G.M. #1 - (1776 - 1799)	116
568.	ECKMAN	Eva Elizabeth	Final	G.M. #1 - (1776 - 1799)	132
569.	EVANS	John	Final	G.M. #1 - (1776 - 1799)	157
570.	ERBAUGH	Balser	Account	G.M. #1 - (1776 - 1799)	360
571.	ERBAUGH	Jacob	Final	G.M. #1 - (1776 - 1799)	467
572.	EASTERDAY	Martin	Account	G.M. #1 - (1776 - 17990	483
573.	EVERLY	Adam	Final	G.M. #1 - (1776 - 1799)	593
574.	ENGLAND	John	Final	G.M. #2 - (1800 - 1805)	40
575.	EBY	Christian	First	G.M. #2 - (1800 - 1805)	200
576.	EVERLY	John	First	G.M. #2 - (1800 - 1805)	231
577.	EBY	Christian	Second	G.M. #2 - (1800 - 1805)	275
578.	EHALT	Elizabeth	Final	G.M. #2 - (1800 - 1805)	358
579.	EBY	Christian	Final	G.M. #2 - (1800 - 1805)	376
580.	EVERLY	John	Final	G.M. #2 - (1800 - 1805)	389
581.	ELDER	Bennett/Bonmit	First	G.M. #2 - (1800 - 1805)	476

582.	ELDER	Charles	First	G.M. #2 - (1800 - 1805)	478
583.	ERB	John	First	R.B. #1 - (1806 - 1809)	8
584.	ELDER	Bennett/Bonnit	Second	R.B. #1 - (1806 - 1809)	20
585.	ELDER	Charles	Second	R.B. #1 - (1806 - 1809)	21
586.	EASTERDAY	Christian	First	R.B. #1 - (1806 - 1809)	179
587.	ELDER	Charles	Final	R.B. #1 - (1806 - 1809)	229
588.	ELDER	Bennett/Bonmit	Final	R.B. #1 - (1806 - 1809)	230
589.	ELDER	Guy	Final	R.B. #1 - (1806 - 1809)	244
590.	EBY	Jacob	First	R.B. #1 - (1806 - 1809)	270
591.	ENSEY	Richard	Final	R.B. #1 - (1806 - 1809)	304
592.	EILER	Frederick	Final	R.B. #1 - (1806 - 1809)	327
593.	ELDER	Guy	Final	R.B. #1 - (1806 - 1809)	353
594.	EVERLY	Peter	First	R.B. #2 - (1809 - 1811)	33
595.	EVERLY	Peter	Final	R.B. #2 - (1809 - 1811)	273
596.	EVANS	James	Final	R.B. #2 - (1809 - 1811)	307
597.	EVERHART	Peter	First	R.B. #2 - (1809 - 1811)	318
598.	ENGLOS	Peter Sr.	Final	R.B. #2 - (1809 - 1811)	335
599.	EBEY	Jacob	2nd & Fl.	R.B. #2 - (1809 - 1811)	473
600.	ENGLER	Jacob	First	R.B. #2 - (1809 - 1811)	478
601.	EVERHART	Peter	Final	R.B. #3 - (1812 - 1815)	57
602.	ECKELS	Michael	1st & Fl..	R.B. #3 - (1812 - 1815)	60
603.	EICHELBERGER	Henry	1st & Fl.	R.B. #3 - (1812 - 1815)	353
604.	ELDER	Frances	1st & Fl.	H.S. #1 - (1815 - 1816)	154
605.	ELLIS	Samuel	1st & Fl.	H.S. #1 - (1815 - 1816)	207
606.	FOUTS	Baltis	Account	A. #1 - (1750 - 1767)	20
607.	FRIEND	Charles	Account	A. #1 - (1750 - 1767)	25
608.	FORTNEY	Henry	Account	A. #1 - (1750 - 1767)	34
609.	FRIEND	Charles	Addl.	A. #1 - (1750 - 1767)	198
610.	FRIEND	Gabriel	Account	A. #1 - (1750 - 1767)	226
611.	FRIEND	Gabriel	Account	A. #1 - (1750 - 1767)	283
612.	FASE/FUSS	Philip	Account	B. #2 - (1768 - 1776)	3
613.	FURNEY	David	Account	B. #2 - (1768 - 1776)	308
614.	FURNEY	David	FInal	B. #2 - (1768 - 1776)	355
615.	FILLER	Balser	Final	B. #2 - (1768 - 1776)	387
616.	FORD	John	Final	B. #2 - (1768 - 1776)	395
617.	FLEMING	Samuel	Final	G.M. #1 - (1777 - 1799)	67
618.	FOUT	Peter	Final	G.M. #1 - (1777 - 1799)	50
619.	FALCONER	Gilbert	Final	G.M. #1 - (1777 - 1799)	86
620.	FICKLE	Michael	Final	G.M. #1 - (1777 - 1799)	149
621.	FERGUSON	Robert	Final	G.M. #1 - (1777 - 1799)	173
622.	FUNK	Henry	Final	G.M. #1 - (1777 - 1799)	174
623.	FOUTS	Balzer	First	G.M. #1 - (1777 - 1799)	204
624.	FISHER	Jacob	Final	G.M. #1 - (1777 - 1799)	216
625.	FIVECOAT	Jacob	Final	G.M. #1 - (1777 - 1799)	220
626.	FARIS	Joseph	Final	G.M. #1 - (1777 - 1799)	237
627.	FRITSPAW	Christian	Final	G.M. #1 - (1777 - 1799)	248
628.	FOGLE	Andrew	Final	G.M. #1 - (1777 - 1799)	315
629.	FROSHOVER	Jacob	Final	G.M. #1 - (1777 - 1799)	354
630.	FREAM	Thomas	Account	G.M. #1 - (1777 - 1799)	356
631.	FREESE	David	Final	G.M. #1 - (1777 - 1799)	420
632.	FLECK	Peter	Account	G.M. #1 - (1777 - 1799)	453
633.	FAIR	Charles	Account	G.M. #1 - (1777 - 1799)	465
634.	FICKLE	Margaret	Account	G.M. #1 - (1777 - 1799)	561

635.	FOUT	Henry	Account		G.M. #1 - (1777 - 1799)	575
636.	FRAZER	Henry	Final		G.M. #1 - (1777 - 1799)	628
637.	FORTNEY	Catharine	Account		G.M. #1 - (1777 - 1799)	643
638.	FORER	Jacob	Final		G.M. #2 - (1800 - 1805)	128
639.	FREDERICK	Jacob	First		G.M. #2 - (1800 - 1805)	147
640.	FOUT	Baltzer	Final		G.M. #2 - (1800 - 1805)	165
641.	FREDERICK	Jacob	Final		G.M. #2 - (1800 - 1805)	171
642.	FORER	Jacob	2nd & Fl.		G.M. #2 - (1800 - 1805)	172
643.	FARTHING	James	First		G.M. #2 - (1800 - 1805)	314
644.	FALKNER	B. John	First		G.M. #2 - (1800 - 1805)	347
645.	FRIEDINGER	Niholas	First		G.M. #2 - (1800 - 1805)	407
646.	FRUSHOUR	Jacob	Final		R.B. #1 - (1806 - 1809)	94
647.	FORNEY	Nicholas	Final		R.B. #1 - (1806 - 1809)	117
648.	FREICK	Philip	Final		R.B. #1 - (1806 - 1809)	265
649.	FLECK	Lucas	Final		R.B. #1 - (1806 - 1809)	286
650.	FRUSHOUR	Jacob	2nd & Fl.		R.B. #1 - (1806 - 1809)	289
651.	FUTTON/FULTON	Robert	First		R.B. #1 - (1806 - 1809)	302
652.	FUTTON/FULTON	Robert	Final		R.B. #1 - (1806 - 1809)	309
653.	FOX	Balser	Final		R.B. #1 - (1806 - 1809)	324
654.	FOREMAN	Jacob	First		R.B. #1 - (1806 - 1809)	388
655.	FOUT	Henry	Final		R.B. #1 - (1806 - 1809)	403
656.	FIRMWALT	Lawrence	Final		R.B. #1 - (1806 - 1809)	425
657.	FRIDDLE	David	First		R.B. #1 - (1806 - 1809)	501
658.	FOX	Peter	Final		R.B. #2 - (1809 - 1811)	11
659.	FRIDDLE	David	Final		R.B. #2 - (1809 - 1811)	25
660.	FOUT	Jacob	First		R.B. #2 - (1809 - 1811)	173
661.	FRUSHOUR	Adam	First		R.B. #2 - (1809 - 1811)	275
662.	FERGUSSON	William	Final		R.B. #2 - (1809 - 1811)	309
663.	FORD	Samuel	First		R.B. #3 - (1812 - 1815)	27
664.	FORD	Samuel	Final		R.B. #3 - (1812 - 1815)	35
665.	FREY	Enoch	First		R.B. #3 - (1812 - 1815)	66
666.	FREY	Enoch	2nd & Fl.		R.B. #3 - (1812 - 1815)	106
667.	FOUT	Henry	2nd & Fl.		R.B. #3 - (1812 - 1815)	218
668.	FOREMAN	Jacob	2nd & Fl.		R.B. #3 - (1812 - 1815)	340
669.	FUNDERBURGH	Walter	First		R.B. #3 - (1812 - 1815)	446
670.	FULKERTH	Hyronemus	1st & Fl.		R.B. #3 - (1812 - 1815)	462
671.	FUNDERBURGH	Walter	2nd & Fl.		H.S. #1 - (1815 - 1816)	43
672.	FREESE	Michael	First		H.S. #1 - (1815 - 1816)	58
673.	FAHS	Abraham	First		H.S. #1 - (1815 - 1816)	106
674.	FRUSHOUR	Adam	Second		H.S. #1 - (1815 - 1816)	109
675.	GRIFFITH	William	Account		A. #1 - (1750 - 1767)	5
676.	GILLASPIE	David	Account		A. #1 - (1750 - 1767)	23
677.	GASSAWAY	John	Account		A. #1 - (1750 - 1767)	57
678.	GROVE	Valentine	Account		A. #1 - (1750 - 1767)	246
679.	GARRISON	Frederick	Account		A. #1 - (1750 - 1767)	339
680.	GIANN	Thomas	Account		B. #2 - (1768 - 1776)	44
681.	GARTRELL	Stephen	Account		B. #2 - (1768 - 1776)	48
682.	GATTON	Richard	Account		B. #2 - (1768 - 1776)	92
683.	GATTON	Richard	Final		B. #2 - (1768 - 1776)	101
684.	GIBSON	William	Final		B. #2 - (1768 - 1776)	174
685.	GOSLING	Ezekiel	Final		B. #2 - (1768 - 1776)	225
686.	GARTRILL	John	Final		B. #2 - (1768 - 1776)	245
687.	GREGG	John	Final		G.M. #1 - (1777 - 1799)	62

688.	GETZENDANNER	Gabriel	Final	G.M. #1 - (1777 - 1799)	64
689.	GRANMER	Martin	Final	G.M. #1 - (1777 - 1799)	89
690.	GREENWOOD	Philip	Final	G.M. #1 - (1777 - 1799)	96
691.	GALT	James	Final	G.M. #1 - (1777 - 1799)	166
692.	GROSSNICKLE	John	Final	G.M. #1 - (1777 - 1799)	170
693.	GUINN	John	Final	G.M. #1 - (1777 - 1799)	171
694.	GETZENDANNER	Adam	Final	G.M. #1 - (1777 - 1799)	180
695.	GILLELAN	John	First	G.M. #1 - (1777 - 1799)	217
696.	GILLELAN	John	Final	G.M. #1 - (1777 - 1799)	221
697.	GOODENBERGH	Casper	Final	G.M. #1 - (1777 - 1799)	241
698.	GOOD	Jacob	Account	G.M. #1 - (1777 - 1799)	307
699.	GRIFFITH	David	Account	G.M. #1 - (1777 - 1799)	335
700.	GROSH	Michael	Account	G.M. #1 - (1777 - 1799)	362
701.	GROVE	Jacob	Final	G.M. #1 - (1777 - 1799)	370
702.	GOOD	Jacob	Account	G.M. #1 - (1777 - 1799)	436
703.	GROSSNICKLE	Peter	Final	G.M. #1 - (1777 - 1799)	440
704.	GASSAWAY	Benjamin	Final	G.M. #1 - (1777 - 1799)	464
705.	GRIFFITH	David	Addl. Fl.	G.M. #1 - (1777 - 1799)	469
706.	GILBERT	Jacob	Account	G.M. #1 - (1777 - 1799)	488
707.	GOOD	George	Account	G.M. #1 - (1777 - 1799)	501
708.	GILBERT	Henry	Account	G.M. #1 - (1777 - 1799)	513
709.	GARNER	Tobias	Account	G.M. #1 - (1777 - 1799)	523
710.	GETTER	Valentine	Account	G.M. #1 - (1777 - 1799)	529
711.	GILBERT	Thomas	Account	G.M. #1 - (1777 - 1799)	577
712.	GILBERT	Thomas	Final	G.M. #1 - (1777 - 1799)	597
713.	GETZENDANNER	Baltis	Final	G.M. #1 - (1777 - 1799)	650
714.	GOOD	George	Final	G.M. #2 - (1800 - 1805)	3
715.	GRIFFITH	David	Final	G.M. #2 - (1800 - 1805)	25
716.	GROFF	John	Account	G.M. #2 - (1800 - 1805)	35
717.	GROSHONG	Elias	Account	G.M. #2 - (1800 - 1805)	66
718.	GRABELL	John	Account	G.M. #2 - (1800 - 1805)	70
719.	GROSH	Conrad	Account	G.M. #2 - (1800 - 1805)	84
720.	GRABELL	John	Final	G.M. #2 - (1800 - 1805)	104
721.	GRIMES	Martin	Final	G.M. #2 - (1800 - 1805)	109
722.	GIST	John	First	G.M. #2 - (1800 - 1805)	126
723.	GAVER	Daniel	First	G.M. #2 - (1800 - 1805)	143
724.	GETZENDANNER	George	First	G.M. #2 - (1800 - 1805)	162
725.	GETTY	Alexander	First	G.M. #2 - (1800 - 1805)	269
726.	GROWER	Varney	Final	G.M. #2 - (1800 - 1805)	335
727.	GROONAMYOR	William	First	G.M. #2 - (1800 - 1805)	399
728.	GAVER	Daniel	Second	G.M. #2 - (1800 - 1805)	405
729.	GAVER	Daniel	Final	G.M. #2 - (1800 - 1805)	414
730.	GROSHON	Elias	First	G.M. #2 - (1800 - 1805)	415
731.	GANTT	John	First	G.M. #2 - (1800 - 1805)	431
732.	GROSHON	Elias	Final	G.M. #2 - (1800 - 1805)	461
734.	GARROTT	Barton	First	R.B. #1 - (1806 - 1809)	18
735.	GANTT	John	Second	R.B. #1 - (1806 - 1809)	91
736.	GETTYS	Alexander	Final	R.B. #1 - (1806 - 1809)	92
737.	GRAVER	Magdelena	Final	R.B. #1 - (1806 - 1809)	145
738.	GARROTT	Barton	Second	R.B. #1 - (1806 - 1809)	206
739.	GIST	John	Second	R.B. #1 - (1806 - 1809)	227
740.	GROVE	Martin	Final	R.B. #1 - (1806 - 1809)	290
741.	GARDNER	Margaret	Final	R.B. #1 - (1806 - 1809)	423

742.	GAITHER	William	Final	R.B. #1 - (1805 - 1809)	460
743.	GARROT	Barton	Final	R.B. #1 - (1805 - 1809)	477
744.	GREENAMYER	William	Second	R.B. #2 - (1809 - 1811)	3
745.	GANTT	Fielder	First	R.B. #2 - (1809 - 1811)	16
746.	GRENAMYER	William	Third	R.B. #2 - (1809 - 1811)	28
747.	GRIM	Daniel	First	R.B. #2 - (1809 - 1811)	29
748.	GISERT	Catharine	Final	R.B. #2 - (1809 - 1811)	69
749.	GOODMAN	William	First	R.B. #2 - (1809 - 1811)	71
750.	GREENWELL	Elizabeth	First	R.B. #2 - (1809 - 1811)	88
751.	GREENWELL	Philip	First	R.B. #2 - (1809 - 1811)	93
752.	GREENWELL	Phillp	Second	R.B. #2 - (1809 - 1811)	119
753..	GARBER	Christian	1st & Fl.	R.B. #2 - (1809 - 1811)	130
754.	GREENWELL	Elizabeth	Final	R.B. #2 - (1809 - 1811)	155
755.	GREENWELL	Philbert	Final	R.B. #2 - (1809 - 1811)	156
756.	GAUGH	Christopher	Final	R.B. #2 - (1809 - 1811)	251
757.	GITTINGS	Erasmus	Final	R.B. #2 - (1809 - 1811)	302
758.	GILBERT	Barnard	First	R.B. #2 - (1809 - 1811)	380
759.	GILBERT	Barnard	Second	R.B. #2 - (1809 - 1811)	415
760.	GIBSON	Thomas	First	R.B. #2 - (1809 - 1811)	446
761.	GRIMES	Nicholas	Final	R.B. #2 - (1809 - 1811)	498
762.	GALLA	Peter	Final	R.B. #3 - (1812 - 1815)	8
763.	GIST	John	3rd & Fl.	R.B. #3 - (1812 - 1815)	78
764.	GILBERT	Barnard	Third	R.B. #3 - (1812 - 1815)	87
765.	GITTINGS	Colmore	1st & Fl.	R.B. #3 - (1812 - 1815)	108
766.	GEBHART	John Jr.	1st & Fl.	R.B. #3 - (1812 - 1815)	127
767.	GEBHART	John Jr.	Second	R.B. #3 - (1812 - 1815)	135
768.	GRABEL	Peter	1st & Fl.	R.B. #3 - (1812 - 1815)	192
769.	GILBERT	Barnard	Fourth	R.B. #3 - (1812 - 1815)	219
770.	GILBERT	Barnard	Fifth	R.B. #3 - (1812 - 1815)	310
771.	GARBER	Martin	1st & Fl.	H.S. #1 - (1815 - 1816)	48
772.	GILBERT	Bernard	Sixth	H.S. #1 - (1815 - 1816)	55
773.	GOOD	Adam	1st & Fl.	H.S. #1 - (1815 - 1816)	93
774.	GARBER	Christian	1st & Fl.	H.S. #1 - (1815 - 1816)	173
775.	HYETT	Seth	Addl.	A. #1 - (1750 - 1767)	10
776.	HUSSEY	John	Account	A. #1 - (1750 - 1767)	14
777.	HARDIN	John	Account	A. #1 - (1750 - 1767)	24
778.	HAYMOND	John	Account	A. #1 - (1750 - 1767)	32
779.	HEDGES	Joseph	Account	A. #1 - (1750 - 1767)	40
780.	HOUSE	John	Account	A. #1 - (1750 - 1767)	42
781.	HYATT	Seth	2nd & Addl.	A. #1 - (1750 - 1767)	78
782.	HOLLAND	James	Account	A. #1 - (1750 - 1767)	82
783.	HIGGINBOTHAM	Charles	Account	A. #1 - (1750 - 1767)	90
784.	HIGGINBOTIIAM	Charles	Addl.	A. #1 - (1750 - 1767)	150
785.	HARRIS	Rachel	Account	A. #1 - (1750 - 1767)	192
786.	HARTLAND	George	Account	A. #1 - (1750 - 1767)	200
787.	HUNTER	Samuel	Account	A. #1 - (1750 - 1767)	217
788.	HARLIN	George	Account	A. #1 - (1750 - 1767)	232
789.	HOLMES	William	Account	A. #1 - (1750 - 1767)	261
790.	HARMAN	Michael	Account	A. #1 - (1750 - 1767)	342
791.	HICKMAN	Henry	Account	A. #1 - (1750 - 1767)	348
792.	HUNT	Henry	Account	A. #1 - (1750 - 1767)	356
793.	HUFNAGLE	Valentine	Account	A. #1 - (1750 - 1767)	379
794.	HILTEBRAND	John	Account	A. #1 - (1750 - 1767)	398

795.	HUFMAN	Jacob	Account	A. #1 - (1750 - 1767)	438
796.	HADMAN	Joseph	Account	A. #1 - (1750 - 1767)	446
797.	HUNTER	Saml. Rev.	Account	B. #2 - (1768 - 1776)	5
798.	HICKMAN	William	Account	B. #2 - (1768 - 1776)	10
799.	HOILE	John	Account	B. #2 - (1768 - 1776)	15
800.	HUFMAN	John	Final	B. #2 - (1768 - 1776)	69
801.	HILTEBRAND	Adam	Final	B. #2 - (1768 - 1776)	91
802.	HAGAR	David	Final	B. #2 - (1768 - 1776)	131
803.	HICKMAN	Joshua Jr.	Final	B. #2 - (1768 - 1776)	143
804.	HARPER	Josiah	Account	B. #2 - (1768 - 1776)	157
805.	HEFNER	Michael	Account	B. #2 - (1768 - 1776)	159
806.	HAINES	Daniel	Account	B. #2 - (1768 - 1776)	179
807.	HAUN	George	Account	B. #2 - (1768 - 1776)	203
808.	HAYES	Zachariah	Account	B. #2 - (1768 - 17760)	230
809.	HAYMOND	Nicholas	Account	B. #2 - (1768 - 1776)	246
810.	HARDMAN	Michael	Account	B. #2 - (1768 - 1776)	277
811.	HUTCHCRAFT	Thomas	Account	B. #2 - (1768 - 1776)	279
812.	HARDING	Elizabeth	Account	B. #2 - (1768 - 1776)	298
813.	HARDMAN	Cathrine	Final	B. #2 - (1768 - 1776)	312
814.	HARRIS	Thomas	Final	B. #2 - (1768 - 1776)	323
815.	HICKMAN	Joshua	Final	B. #2 - (1768 - 1776)	338
816.	HORINE	Tobias	Account	B. #2 - (1768 - 1776)	339
817.	HAWKINS	John	Final	B. #2 - (1768 - 1776)	373
818.	HARGARIDER	Jno.	Final	B. #2 - (1768 - 1776)	376
819.	HICKMAN	David	Final	B. #2 - (1768 - 1776)	386
820.	HEARSE	Coonrod	Account	G.M. #1 - (1777 - 1799)	11
821.	HUTSELL	George	Account	G.M. #1 - (1777 - 1799)	21
822.	HUMMER	Jacob	Account	G.M. #1 - (1777 - 1799)	40
823.	HEMP.	Nicholas	Account	G.M. #1 - (1777 - 1799)	43
824.	HUFFMAN	Peter	Account	G.M. #1 - (1777 - 1799)	53
825.	HEDGES	Moses	Final	G.M. #1 - (1777 - 1799)	98
826.	HINKERLY	Frederick	Final	G.M. #1 - (1777 - 1799)	103
827.	HUMMELL	John	Final	G.M. #1 - (1777 - 17990)	104
828.	HEDGE	William	Final	G.M. #1 - (1777 - 1799)	109
829.	HAGER	Alexander	Final	G.M. #1 - (1777 - 1799)	126
830.	HOFFIN	Elizabeth	Final	G.M. #1 - (1777 - 1799)	144
831.	HARTSOKE	Margaret	Final	G.M. #1 - (1777 - 1799)	147
832.	HARTSOKE	Peter	Final	G.M. #1 - (1777 - 1799)	148
833.	HAGAR	John	Final	G.M. #1 - (1777 - 1799)	162
834.	HARDESTY	George	Final	G.M. #1 - (1777 - 1799)	185
835.	HOOVER	Nicholas	Final	G.M. #1 - (1777 - 1799)	194
836.	HUMBERT	William	Account	G.M. #1 - (1777 - 1799)	203
837.	HALL	Edward	First	G.M. #1 - (1777 - 1799)	208
838.	HARDING	Philip	Final	G.M. #1 - (1777 - 1799)	214
839.	HORINE	Tobias	Account	G.M. #1 - (1777 - 1799)	216
840.	HORINE	Tobias	Account	G.M. #1 - (1777 - 1799)	236
841.	HAMMOND	Thomas	Final	G.M. #1 - (1777 - 1799)	240
842.	HILDEBRAND	Nicholas	Final	G.M. #1 - (1777 - 1799)	255
843.	HAWN	Michael	Account	G.M. #1 - (1777 - 1799)	265
844.	HALLIDAY	James	First	G.M. #1 - (1777 - 1799)	303
845.	HART	Valentine	Final	G.M. #1 - (1777 - 1799)	304
846.	HARLON	John	Final	G.M. #1 - (1777 - 1799)	319
847.	HUFFORD	Christian	Final	G.M. #1 - (1777 - 1799)	329

848.	HAMMER	Andrew	Final	G.M. #1 - (1777 - 1799)	333
849.	HALL	Edward	Second	G.M. #1 - (1777 - 1799)	338
850.	HALL	Edward	Final	G.M. #1 - (1777 - 1799)	369
851.	HAWN	Michael	Second	G.M. #1 - (1777 - 1799)	373
852.	HOCKMAN	Abraham	Account	G.M. #1 - (1777 - 1799)	393
853.	HOWARD	Cornelius	Account	G.M. #1 - (1777 - 1799)	396
854.	HARGARADER	Mary	Account	G.M. #1 - (1777 - 1799)	399
855.	HAWN	Michael	Final	G.M. #1 - (1777 - 1799)	445
856.	HEDGES	Peter	Final	G.M. #1 - (1777 - 1799)	461
856A.	HAMMETT	Robert	Final	G.M. #1 - (1777 - 1799)	472
857.	HYFIELD	Jonathan	Account	G.M. #1 - (1777 - 1799)	481
858.	HYFIELD	Jonathan	Final	G.M. #1 - (1777 - 1799)	483
859.	HAVERLY	Michael	Account	G.M. #1 - (1777 - 1799)	484
860.	HAYSE	Jonathan	Account	G.M. #1 - (1777 - 1799)	503
861.	HOLTS	Benedict	Account	G.M. #1 - (1777 - 1799)	506
862.	HAYSE	Jonathan	Second	G.M. #1 - (1777 - 1799)	511
863.	HUFFORD	Philip	Account	G.M. #1 - (1777 - 1799)	516
864.	HOLLAND	Richard	Account	G.M. #1 - (1777 - 1799)	520
865.	HARDMAN	Henry	Account	G.M. #1 - (1777 - 1799)	531
866.	HANE	Jacob	Final	G.M. #1 - (1777 - 1799)	542
867.	HARPE	John	Account	G.M. #1 - (1777 - 1799)	551
868.	HALL	Joseph	Account	G.M. #1 - (1777 - 1799)	563
869.	HILL	Robert	Account	G.M. #1 - (1777 - 1799)	585
870.	HELM	Francis N.	Account	G.M. #1 - (1777 - 1799)	587
871.	HAWN	Michael	Final	G.M. #1 - (1777 - 1799)	604
872.	HEDGES	Charles	Final	G.M. #1 - (1777 - 1799)	616
872A.	HECK	Balser	Account	G.M. #1 - (1777 - 1799)	617
873.	HOCKMAN	Jacob	Final	G.M. #1 - (1777 - 1799)	625
874.	HAYSE	Jonathan	Third	G.M. #1 - (1777 - 1799)	667
875.	HUFFORD	Philip	Final	G.M. #2 - (1800 - 1805)	13
876.	HOY	Nicholas	First	G.M. #2 - (1800 - 1805)	18
877.	HOBBS	Nicholas	First	G.M. #2 - (1800 - 1805)	19
878.	HILL	Abraham	Final	G.M. #2 - (1800 - 1805)	67
879.	HOBBS	John	Account	G.M. #2 - (1800 - 1805)	72
880.	HOCKENSMITH	George	Final	G.M. #2 - (1800 - 1805)	76
881.	HOBBS	Nicholas	Final	G.M. #2 - (1800 - 1805)	93
882.	HERSHBERGER	Bernard	Final	G.M. #2 - (1800 - 1805)	110
883.	HYNER	William	Final	G.M. #2 - (1800 - 1805)	157
884.	HAUSER	Hennick	Final	G.M. #2 - (1800 - 1805)	197
885.	HOUPMAN	Tetrick John	Final	G.M. #2 - (1800 - 1805)	202
886.	HOLLAR	George	Final	G.M. #2 - (1800 - 1805)	217
887.	HAGAN	Hugh	First	G.M. #2 - (1800 - 1805)	259
888.	HILL	Joseph	First	G.M. #2 - (1800 - 1805)	266
889.	HAMMER	Francis	Final	G.M. #2 - (1800 - 1805)	341
890.	HIGDON	John	Final	G.M. #2 - (1800 - 1805)	344
891.	HERD	Jacob	Final	G.M. #2 - (1800 - 1805)	354
892.	HAGAN	Hugh	Second	G.M. #2 - (1800 - 1805)	366
893.	HART	Adam	Final	G.M. #2 - (1800 - 1805)	441
894.	HITESHEW	Jacob	Final	G.M. #2 - (1800 - 1805)	445
895.	HAWN	Michael	Final	G.M. #2 - (1800 - 1805)	462
896.	HOWARD	Cornelius	Final	G.M. #2 - (1800 - 1805)	482
897.	HOWARD	George	Final	R.B. #1 - (1806 - 1809)	12
898.	HAWN	Leonard	First	R.B. #1 - (1806 - 1809)	24

No.	Surname	Given	Type	Reference	Page
899.	HARDING	Charles	Final	R.B. #1 - (1806 - 1809)	72
900.	HARMON	Marks	First	R.B. #1 - (1806 - 1809)	85
901.	HOSPLOHORN	Ludwick	Final	R.B. #1 - (1806 - 1809)	138
902.	HAWN	Leonard	Final	R.B. #1 - (1806 - 1809)	173
903.	HARRIS	George	1st & Fl.	R.B. #1 - (1806 - 1809)	185
904.	HILL	Margaret	First	R.B. #1 - (1806 - 1809)	195
905.	HILL	Margaret	Final	R.B. #1 - (1806 - 1809)	202
906.	HOWARD	Joseph	First	R.B. #1 - (1806 - 1809)	251
907.	HINER	Herbert	First	R.B. #1 - (1806 - 1809)	343
908.	HYDE	Jonathan	Final	R.B. #1 - (1806 - 1809)	355
909.	HILDEBRICK	George	Final	R.B. #2 - (1806 - 1809)	48
910.	HOLTZAPPLE	Mary	Final	R.B. #2 - (1806 - 1809)	55
911.	HILL	Joseph	Final	R.B. #2 - (1806 - 1809)	101
912.	HINER	Herbert	Final	R.B. #2 - (1806 - 1809)	147
913.	HOMES	Thomas	First	R.B. #2 - (1806 - 1809)	158
914.	HOMES	Thomas	Final	R.B. #2 - (1806 - 1809)	176
915.	HOOVER	Christian	First	R.B. #2 - (1806 - 1809)	198
916.	HITESHEW	Nicholas	First	R.B. #2 - (1806 - 1809)	401
917.	HILDERBRAND	Jacob	First	R.B. #2 - (1806 - 1809)	465
918.	HOWELL	Stephen	Final	R.B. #2 - (1806 - 1809)	482
919.	HITESHEW	Nicholas	Second	R.B. #2 - (1806 - 1809)	492
920.	HOOPER	Abraham	First	R.B. #3 - (1812 - 1815)	32
921.	HALL	James	1st & Fl.	R.B. #3 - (1812 - 1815)	90
922.	HAUER	Nicholas	First	R.B. #3 - (1812 - 1815)	94
923.	HAMMOND	John	First	R.B. #3 - (1812 - 1815)	113
924.	HILL	Zephaniah	First	R.B. #3 - (1812 - 1815)	149
925.	HERSHBERGER	Henry	First	R.B. #3 - (1812 - 1815)	151
926.	HERSHBERGER	Henry	2nd & Fl.	R.B. #3 - (1812 - 1815)	161
927.	HARTSOCK	Henry	1st & Fl.	R.B. #3 - (1812 - 1815)	165
928.	HEFFNER	Fred. Jacob	First	R.B. #3 - (1812 - 1815)	189
929.	HILLEARY	Thomas	1st & Fl.	R.B. #3 - (1812 - 1815)	210
930.	HAMMOND	John	Second	R.B. #3 - (1812 - 1815)	227
931.	HAWK	Peter	First	R.B. #3 - (1812 - 1815)	232
932.	HAGAN	Hugh	Third	R.B. #3 - (1812 - 1815)	243
933.	HAGAN	Hugh	4th & Fl.	R.B. #3 - (1812 - 1815)	255
934.	HAMILTON	John	1st & Fl.	R.B. #3 - (1812 - 1815)	262
935.	HANN	Henry	1st & Fl.	R.B. #3 - (1812 - 1815)	278
936.	HAUER	Nicholas	2nd & Fl.	R.B. #3 - (1812 - 1815)	287
937.	HARBAUGH	Ludwick	1st & Fl.	R.B. #3 - (1812 - 1815)	307
938.	HALL	Francis	1st & Fl.	R.B. #3 - (1812 - 1815)	326
939.	HALL	Benjamin	First	R.B. #3 - (1812 - 1815)	330
940.	HARGATE	Peter	First	R.B. #3 - (1812 - 1815)	342
941.	HILDERBRAND	Jacob	2nd & Fl.	R.B. #3 - (1812 - 1815)	348
942.	HOUSE	George Jr.	1st & Fl.	R.B. #3 - (1812 - 1815)	399
943.	HUSTON	Thomas	1st & Fl.	R.B. #3 - (1812 - 1815)	411
944.	HILL	Abraham	1st & Fl.	R.B. #3 - (1812 - 1815)	424
945.	HAFF	Abraham Jr.	First	R.B. #3 - (1812 - 1815)	428
946.	HAFF	Abraham Jr.	Second	R.B. #3 - (1812 - 1815)	455
947.	HERRING	Ludwick	First	H.S. #1 - (1815 - 1816)	4
948.	HANN	Ludwick	1st & Fl.	H.S. #1 - (1815 - 1816)	29
949.	HARGATE	Peter	2nd & Fl.	H.S. #1 - (1815 - 1816)	33
950.	HAMMOND	John	3rd & Fl.	H.S. #1 - (1815 - 1816)	66
951.	HEFFNER	Jacob Fredk.	2nd	H.S. #1 - (1815 - 1816)	110

952.	HERRING	Ludwick	2nd & Fl.	H.S. #1 - (1815 - 1816)	121
953.	HITESHEW	William	First	H.S. #1 - (1815 - 1816)	152
954.	HILLEARY	Ann	First	H.S. #1 - (1815 - 1816)	171
955.	HOWARD	Joseph	2nd & Fl.	H.S. #1 - (1815 - 1816)	201
956.	HITESHEW	William	2nd & Fl.	H.S. #1 - (1815 - 1816)	203
957.	HILLEARY	Ann	2nd & Fl.	H.S. #1 - (1815 - 1816)	206
958.	HAFF	Abraham Jr.	Fourth	H.S. #1 - (1815 - 1816)	219
959.	HAUBERT	Elizabeth	1st & Fl.	H.S. #1 - (1815 - 1816)	231
960.	HAUBERT	Mary Eve	1st & Fl.	H.S. #1 - (1815 - 1816)	234
961.	HUGHES	Jesse	1st & Fl.	H.S. #1 - (1815 - 1816)	259
962.	ILGNER	Christian	Account	G.M. #1 - (1777 - 1799)	22
963.	IJAMS	Plummer	Account	G.M. #1 - (1777 - 1799)	606
964.	IJAMS	Plummer	Second	G.M. #2 - (1800 - 1805)	17
965.	ISENBURGH	Gabriel	First	G.M. #2 - (1800 - 1805)	178
966.	IJAMS	Richard	First	R.B. #1 - (1806 - 1809)	137
967.	IJAMS	Richard	Final	R.B. #1 - (1806 - 1809)	307
968.	JACKS	John	Account	A. #1 - (1750 - 1767)	179
969.	JONES	John	Account	A. #1 - (1750 - 1767)	297
970.	JOHNSON	John	Account	A. #1 - (1750 - 1767)	323
971.	JOHNSON	Edward	Account	A. #1 - (1750 - 1767)	350
972.	JENKINS	Josiah	Account	A. #1 - (1750 - 1767)	382
973.	JESSERANG	Bartholomew	Account	A. #1 - (1750 - 1767)	424
974.	JOHNSON	James	Account	B. #2 - (1768 - 1776)	76
975.	JEWELL	George	Final	B. #2 - (1768 - 1776)	115
976.	JOHNSON	Thos.	Final	B. #2 - (1768 - 1776)	213
977.	JONES	Josias	Final	B. #2 - (1768 - 1776)	318
978.	JONES	Thomas	Final	B. #2 - (1768 - 1776)	320
979.	JOHNSON	Thomas	Final	G.M. #1 - (1777 - 1799)	58
980.	JOHNSON	John	Final	G.M. #1 - (1777 - 1799)	94
981.	JOHNSON	Thomas	Final	G.M. #1 - (1777 - 1799)	126
982.	JOHNSON	Joseph	Final	G.M. #1 - (1777 - 1799)	215
983.	JOLLAGH	Frederick	Account	G.M. #1 - (1777 - 1799)	278
984.	JUSTICE	John	Account	G.M. #1 - (1777 - 1799)	324
985.	JUSTICE	John	Final	G.M. #1 - (1777 - 1799)	324
986.	JENINGS	Richard	Account	G.M. #1 - (1777 - 1799)	574
987.	JUSTICE	John	Final	G.M. #2 - (1800 - 1805)	29
988.	JACOBS	George	Final	G.M. #2 - (1800 - 1805)	52
989.	JACOB	Daniel	Final	G.M. #2 - (1800 - 1805)	159
990.	JACOBS	Benjamin	Final	G.M. #2 - (1800 - 1805)	184
991.	JUDA	Jacob	Final	G.M. #2 - (1800 - 1805)	330
992.	JUDA	Philip	First	G.M. #2 - (1800 - 1805)	360
993.	JENKINS	John	Final	G.M. #2 - (1800 - 1805)	468
994.	JUDA	Philip	Final	R.B. #1 - (1806 - 1809)	70
995.	JAMISON	Henry	First	R.B. #1 - (1806 - 1809)	111
996.	JAMISON	Henry	Second	R.B. #1 - (1806 - 1809)	126
997.	JAMISON	John	First	R.B. #1 - (1806 - 1809)	128
998.	JAMISON	John	Second	R.B. #1 - (1806 - 1809)	150
999.	JAMISON	Henry	Third	R.B. #1 - (1806 - 18090)	184
1000.	JOHNSON	Thomas	1st & Fl.	R.B. #1 - (1806 - 1809)	224
1001.	JOHNSON	Joseph	1st & Fl.	R.B. #1 - (1806 - 1809)	279
1002.	JAMISON	Henry	Fourth	R.B. #1 - (1806 - 1809)	357
1003.	JAMISON	Henry	Fifth	R.B. #1 - (1806 - 1809)	364
1004.	JAMISON	Henry	Final	R.B. #1 - (1806 - 1809)	365

1005.	JAMISON	John	Final	R.B. #1 - (1806 - 1809)	393
1006.	JOHNSON	John	1st & Fl.	R.B. #2 - (1809 - 1811)	363
1007.	JOHNSON	Baker	First	R.B. #3 - (1812 - 1815)	74
1008.	JOHNSON	J. Thomas	1st & Fl.	R.B. #3 - (1812 - 1815)	299
1009.	JOHNSON	William	1st & Fl.	H.S. #1 - (1815 - 1816)	16
1010.	KELLY	Samuel	Account	A. #1 - (1750 - 1767)	28
1011.	KERN	Jacob	Account	A. #1 - (1750 - 1767)	111
1012.	KEEN	Henry	Account	A. #1 - (1750 - 1767)	164
1013.	KITTS	George	Account	A. #1 - (1750 - 1767)	178
1014.	KEPLINGER	George	Account	A. #1 - (1750 - 1767)	331
1015.	KEMP	John	Account	A. #1 - (1750 - 1767)	346
1016.	KELLER	Jacob	Final	B. #2 - (1768 - 1776)	118
1017.	KELLER	Abraham	Final	B. #2 - (1768 - 1776)	171
1018.	KIMBERLIN	Mathias	Final	B. #2 - (1768 - 1776)	269
1019.	KELLER	Rudolph	Final	B. #2 - (1768 - 1776)	361
1020.	KIMBOL	John	Account	G.M. #1 - (1777 - 1799)	2
1021.	KIMBOL	Lettice	Account	G.M. #1 - (1777 - 1799)	3
1022.	KELLER	Rudolph	First	G.M. #1 - (1777 - 1799)	16
1023.	KELLER	Rudolph	Second	G.M. #1 - (1777 - 1799)	17
1024.	KUNU/KUNCE	Philip	Account	G.M. #1 - (1777 - 1799)	33
1025.	KING	Philip	Account	G.M. #1 - (1777 - 1799)	38
1026.	KETULDY	Conrod	Account	G.M. #1 - (1777 - 1799)	39
1027.	KEMP	Nicholas	Account	G.M. #1 - (1777 - 1799)	43
1028.	KELP	Philip	Account	G.M. #1 - (1777 - 1799)	50
1029.	KNOUFF	Margaret	Account	G.M. #1 - (1777 - 1799)	74
1030.	KEIN	Joseph	Final	G.M. #1 - (1777 - 1799)	121
1031.	KING	Abraham	Final	G.M. #1 - (1777 - 1799)	168
1032.	KESSLER	Jacob	Final	G.M. #1 - (1777 - 1799)	189
1033.	KERN	Michael	Final	G.M. #1 - (1777 - 1799)	199
1034.	KENSLER	Jacob	Final	G.M. #1 - (1777 - 1799)	202
1035.	KILE	Adam	Final	G.M. #1 - (1777 - 1799)	206
1036.	KILE	Elizabeth	Final	G.M. #1 - (1777 - 1799)	207
1037.	KIPPS	Abraham	Final	G.M. #1 - (1777 - 1799)	285
1038.	KING	Andrew	Account	G.M. #1 - (1777 - 1799)	379
1039.	KEMP	Jacob	Account	G.M. #1 - (1777 - 1799)	407
1040.	KELLER	Rudolph	Third	G.M. #1 - (1777 - 1799)	415
1041.	KIBLER	Michael	Account	G.M. #1 - (1777 - 1799)	435
1042.	KAYCOP	Frederick	Account	G.M. #1 - (1777 - 1799)	452
1043.	KERR	Hugh	Final	G.M. #1 - (1777 - 1799)	458
1044.	KOELER	Jacob	Account	G.M. #1 - (1777 - 1799)	462
1045.	KEMP	David	Account	G.M. #1 - (1777 - 1799)	550
1046.	KNIGHT	William	Account	G.M. #1 - (1777 - 1799)	618
1047.	KITTAMAN	George	Final	G.M. #2 - (1800 - 1805)	28
1048.	KEPLER	Jacob	Account	G.M. #2 - (1800 - 1805)	85
1049.	KEMP	Henry	Final	G.M. #2 - (1800 - 1805)	131
1050.	KERR	Agness	Final	G.M. #2 - (1800 - 1805)	216
1051.	KOONTZ	Henry	Final	G.M. #2 - (1800 - 1805)	291
1052.	KEMP	John	First	G.M. #2 - (1800 - 1805)	296
1053.	KNOUF	Jacob	First	G.M. #2 - (1800 - 1805)	299
1054.	KEMP	Henry	2nd & Fl.	G.M. #2 - (1800 - 1805)	302
1055.	KELLER	George	First	G.M. #2 - (1800 - 1805)	364
1056.	KEMP	John	Final	G.M. #2 - (1800 - 1805)	375
1057.	KELLER	George	Final	G.M. #2 - (1800 - 1805)	412

1058.	KEPHART	Simon	Final	G.M. #2 - (1800 - 1805)	447
1059.	KELLER	Jacob	Final	R.B. #1 - (1806 - 1809)	50
1060.	KELLER	Barbara	Final	R.B. #1 - (1806 - 1809)	52
1061.	KEMP	Ludwick	First	R.B. #1 - (1806 - 1809)	67
1062.	KEEFER	Frederick	Final	R.B. #1 - (1806 - 1809)	78
1063.	KELLER	Jacob Jr.	Final	R.B. #1 - (1806 - 1809)	96
1064.	KEMP	Ludwick	Final	R.B. #1 - (1806 - 1809)	140
1065.	KEPHART	Solomon	First	R.B. #1 - (1806 - 1809)	171
1066.	KARN	Frederick	First	R.B. #1 - (1806 - 1809)	207
1067.	KARN	Frederick	Final	R.B. #1 - (1806 - 1809)	250
1068.	KEPHART	Solomon	Second	R.B. #1 - (1806 - 1809)	489
1069.	KREGLOE	Elizabeth	First	R.B. #2 - (1809 - 1811)	1
1070.	KREGLOE	Elizabeth	Final	R.B. #2 - (1809 - 1811)	10
1071.	KNOUF	Jacob	Second	R.B. #2 - (1809 - 1811)	37
1072.	KIRTZ	George	First	R.B. #2 - (1809 - 1811)	47
1073.	KELLER	Philip	First	R.B. #2 - (1809 - 1811)	289
1074.	KEMP	Peter Sr.	Final	R.B. #2 - (1809 - 1811)	324
1075.	KEMP	Philip	1st & Fl.	R.B. #2 - (1809 - 1811)	362
1076.	KEEFER	Ludwick	Final	R.B. #2 - (1809 - 1811)	376
1077.	KEEVER	Andrew	1st & Fl.	R.B. #2 - (1809 - 1811)	450
1078.	KEMP	Peter	First	R.B. #2 - (1809 - 1811)	486
1079.	KRISE	Henry	Final	R.B. #3 - (1812 - 1815)	55
1080.	KEMP	Peter	Second	R.B. #3 - (1812 - 1815)	58
1081.	KITZMILLER	Elizabeth	Final	R.B. #3 - (1812 - 1815)	62
1082.	KEMP	Peter	3rd & Fl.	R.B. #3 - (1812 - 1815)	143
1083.	KNOX	John	First	R.B. #3 - (1812 - 1815)	146
1084.	KEEFER	Margaret	1st & Fl.	R.B. #3 - (1812 - 1815)	265
1085.	KELLER	Philip John	First	R.B. #3 - (1812 - 1815)	285
1086.	KELLER	Philip John	2nd & Fl.	R.B. #3 - (1812 - 1815)	292
1087.	KNOX	John	2nd & Fl.	R.B. #3 - (1812 - 1815)	317
1088.	KESSLER	Mathew	1st & Fl.	R.B. #3 - (1812 - 1815)	402
1089.	KINKERLY	Frederick	First	R.B. #3 - (1812 - 1815)	409
1090.	KEPHART	Solomon	Third	R.B. #3 - (1812 - 1815)	443
1091.	KELLER	John	1st & Fl.	H.S. #1 - (1815 - 1816)	24
1092.	KARN	Magdalena	1st & Fl.	H.S. #1 - (1815 - 1816)	27
1093.	KINLEY	Jacob	First	H.S. #1 - (1815 - 1816)	46
1094.	KNOUF	Jacob	3rd & Fl.	H.S. #1 - (1815 - 1816)	52
1095.	KNOUF	John	1st & Fl.	H.S. #1 - (1815 - 1816)	92
1096.	KOONS	Paul	1st & Fl.	H.S. #1 - (1815 - 1816)	263
1097.	LEMAR	Thomas	Account	A. #1 - (1750 - 1767)	1
1098.	LYNHAM	Bartholomew	Account	A. #1 - (1750 - 1767)	235
1099.	LONG	David	Account	A. #1 - (1750 - 1767)	308
1100.	LOY	George	Account	A. #1 - (1750 - 1767)	385
1101.	LAYMAN	Christopher	Account	A. #1 - (1750 - 1767)	387
1102.	LITTON	Caleb	Account	A. #1 - (1750 - 1767)	414
1103.	LOVELESS	Baptist John	Account	A. #1 - (1750 - 1767)	421
1104.	LOY	Jacob	Account	A. #1 - (1750 - 1767)	449
1105.	LOFLIN	Richard	Final	B. #2 - (1768 - 1776)	137
1106.	LITTLE	John	Final	B. #2 - (1768 - 1776)	139
1107.	LIGHT	Philip/Peter	Final	B. #2 - (1768 - 1776)	200
1108.	LIGHTER	Melchor	Final	B. #2 - (1768 - 1776)	345
1109.	LANEY	Mathew	Final	B. #2 - (1768 - 1776)	353
1110.	LIGHTY	Jacob	Final	B. #2 - (1768 - 1776)	359

#	Surname	Given	Type	Reference	Page
1111.	LITTLE	Peter	Final	B. #2 - (1768 - 1776)	364
1112.	LINGENFELTER	John	Account	G.M. #1 - (1777 - 1799)	18
1113.	LITTLE	John	Account	G.M. #1 - (1777 - 1799)	47
1114.	LONG	Thomas	Final	G.M. #1 - (1777 - 1799)	100
1115.	LICKLIDER	Conrod	Final	G.M. #1 - (1777 - 1799)	106
1116.	LYNN	David	Final	G.M. #1 - (1777 - 1799)	127
1117.	LOHR	John	Final	G.M. #1 - (1777 - 1799)	139
1118.	LAYMAN	Philip Jacob	Final	G.M. #1 - (1777 - 1799)	141
1119.	LEESE	Philip	Final	G.M. #1 - (1777 - 1799)	151
1120.	LAWRENCE	John	Final	G.M. #1 - (1777 - 1799)	154
1121.	LAWRENCE	John	Final	G.M. #1 - (1777 - 1799)	182
1122.	LAMBERT	Baker	Final	G.M. #1 - (1777 - 1799)	184
1123.	LINEBAUGH	Frederick	Final	G.M. #1 - (1777 - 1799)	267
1124.	LINEBAUGH	Frederick	Final	G.M. #1 - (1777 - 1799)	298
1125.	LAYMAN	John	Final	G.M. #1 - (1777 - 1799)	455
1126.	LABO	Abraham	Final	G.M. #1 - (1777 - 1799)	478
1127.	LUCKETT	John	Account	G.M. #1 - (1777 - 1799)	509
1128.	LIVERS	Robert	Account	G.M. #1 - (1777 - 1799)	518
1129.	LUTZ	George	Account	G.M. #1 - (1777 - 1799)	526
1130.	LIVERS	Robert	Final	G.M. #1 - (1777 - 1799)	530
1131.	LEESE	Conrod	First	G.M. #1 - (1777 - 1799)	642
1132.	LAMBKEY	Wm. Christian	First	G.M. #2 - (1800 - 1805)	122
1133.	LYLES	William	First	G.M. #2 - (1800 - 1805)	156
1134.	LEFAVER	Christian	Final	G.M. #2 - (1800 - 1805)	161
1135.	LOW	Andrew	Final	G.M. #2 - (1800 - 1805)	205
1136.	LAWRENCE	Martha	Final	G.M. #2 - (1800 - 1805)	222
1137.	LAKIN	Abraham	First	G.M. #2 - (1800 - 1805)	255
1138.	LESHORN	Paul	Final	G.M. #2 - (1800 - 1805)	271
1139.	LIVERS	Henry	First	G.M. #2 - (1800 - 1805)	276
1140.	LEWIS	Thomas	Final	G.M. #2 - (1800 - 1805)	343
1141.	LINTON	William	Final	G.M. #2 - (1800 - 1805)	350
1142.	LIVERS	Henry	Final	G.M. #2 - (1800 - 1805)	362
1143.	LEFAVER	Elias	First	G.M. #2 - (1800 - 1805)	373
1144.	LAWRENCE	Richard	First	G.M. #2 - (1800 - 1805)	380
1145.	LAMAR	John	Final	G.M. #2 - (1800 - 1805)	392
1146.	LEFAVER	Elias	Final	G.M. #2 - (1800 - 1805)	424
1147.	LINTON	Zachariah	First	G.M. #2 - (1800 - 1805)	467
1148.	LAKIN	Abraham	Final	G.M. #2 - (1800 - 1805)	475
1149.	LEISTER	Nicholas	Final	R.B. #1 - (1806 - 1809)	3
1150.	LONG	Ludwick	Final	R.B. #1 - (1806 - 1809)	13
1151.	LYLES	William	Second	R.B. #1 - (1806 - 1809)	17
1152.	LEAPLEY	Peter	First	R.B. #1 - (1806 - 1809)	45
1153.	LONG	Frederick	Final	R.B. #1 - (1806 - 1809)	46
1154.	LAMBKEY	Wm. Christian	Second	R.B. #1 - (1806 - 1809)	57
1155.	LONG	John	First	R.B. #1 - (1806 - 1809)	73
1156.	LOOKENPEEL	Jacob	Final	R.B. #1 - (1806 - 1809)	131
1157.	LEVY	David Sr.	First	R.B. #1 - (1806 - 1809)	187
1158.	LEVY	David Sr.	First	R.B. #1 - (1806 - 1809)	233
1159.	LYLES	William	Third	R.B. #1 - (1806 - 1809)	262
1160.	LYLES	William	Final	R.B. #1 - (1806 - 1809)	267
1161.	LEVY	David Sr.	Second	R.B. #1 - (1806 - 1809)	298
1162.	LAMBKEY	Wm. Christian	Third	R.B. #1 - (1806 - 1809)	313
1163.	LEVY	David Jr.	Second	R.B. #1 - (1806 - 1809)	406

No.	Surname	Given	Type	Reference	Page
1164.	LAWRENCE	Richard	Second	R.B. #1 - (1806 - 1809)	407
1165.	LINGANFELTER	Valentine	First	R.B. #2 - (1809 - 1811)	40
1166.	LIVERS	William	First	R.B. #2 - (1809 - 1811)	56
1167.	LEVY	David Sr.	Third	R.B. #2 - (1809 - 1811)	85
1168.	LINTON	Zachariah	Final	R.B. #2 - (1809 - 1811)	91
1169.	LAWRENCE	Richard	Third	R.B. #2 - (1809 - 1811)	96
1170.	LETT	Daniel	First	R.B. #2 - (1809 - 1811)	284
1171.	LEVY	Jacob	First	R.B. #2 - (1809 - 1811)	320
1172.	LONG	Conrad	Final	R.B. #2 - (1809 - 1811)	328
1173.	LEATHER	John	Final	R.B. #2 - (1809 - 1811)	330
1174.	LOHRA	John	Final	R.B. #2 - (1809 - 1811)	332
1175.	LAMBERT	John	First	R.B. #2 - (1809 - 1811)	448
1176.	LAWRENCE	Richard	Fourth	R.B. #3 - (1812 - 1815)	67
1177.	LONG	Christopher	First	R.B. #3 - (1812 - 1815)	117
1178.	LONG	Mary	1st & Fl.	R.B. #3 - (1812 - 1815)	137
1179.	LEMAR	B. William	1st & Fl.	R.B. #3 - (1812 - 1815)	246
1180.	LEACH	Edward	First	R.B. #3 - (1812 - 1815)	263
1181.	LEVY	Jacob	Second	R.B. #3 - (1812 - 1815)	283
1182.	LEVY	Valentine	1st & Fl.	R.B. #3 - (1812 - 1815)	288
1183.	LONG	Christopher	Second	R.B. #3 - (1812 - 1815)	291
1184.	LEACH	Edward	2nd & Fl.	R.B. #3 - (1812 - 1815)	333
1185.	LEVY	David Sr.	1st & Fl.	R.B. #3 - (1812 - 1815)	356
1186.	LEVY	Samuel	First	R.B. #3 - (1812 - 1815)	377
1187.	LONG	Christopher	3rd & Fl.	R.B. #3 - (1812 - 1815)	400
1188.	LYNCH	Mary	1st & Fl.	R.B. #3 - (1812 - 1815)	432
1189.	MELOTT	Theodore	Account	A. #1 - (1750 - 1767)	39
1190.	MONG	Godfrey	Account	A. #1 - (1750 - 1767)	54
1191.	MONG	Godfrey	Account	A. #1 - (1750 - 1767)	100
1192.	MARKLAND	Margarett	Account	A. #1 - (1750 - 1767)	115
1193.	MAGRUDER	Ninian	Account	A. #1 - (1750 - 1767)	117
1194.	MAGRUDER	Ninian	Account	A. #1 - (1750 - 17670	148
1195.	MILLER	Abraham	Account	A. #1 - (1750 - 1767)	169
1196.	MILLHOUSE	Morris	Account	A. #1 - (1750 - 1767)	171
1197.	MAGRUDER	Alexander	Account	A. #1 - (1750 - 1767)	185
1198.	MANTZ	Peter	Account	A. #1 - (1750 - 1767)	203
1199.	MANTZ	Peter	Addl.	A. #1 - (1750 - 1767)	206
1200.	MUSSELMAN	Mathias	Account	A. #1 - (1750 - 1767)	206
1201.	MATHEWS	Chidley	Account	A. #1 - (1750 - 1767)	258
1202.	McSWAIN	George	Account	A. #1 - (1750 - 1767)	284
1203.	MEYRICK	Richard	Account	A. #1 - (1750 - 1767)	293
1204.	MATHEWS	Edward	Account	A. #1 - (1750 - 1767)	409
1205.	MILES	Thos.	Account	B. #2 - (1768 - 1776)	57
1206.	MATHEWS	Jno.	Final	B. #2 - (1768 - 1776)	120
1207.	MOCKBEE	Lucy	Final	B. #2 - (1768 - 1776)	173
1208.	MASTERS	Robert	Final	B. #2 - (1768 - 1776)	222
1209.	MULLENDORE	Jacob	Final	B. #2 - (1768 - 1776)	226
1210.	MACKALL	Benjamin	Final	B. #2 - (1768 - 1776)	231
1211.	MACKATEE	William	Final	B. #2 - (1768 - 1776)	259
1212.	MATHEWS	Samuel	Final	B. #2 - (1768 - 1776)	260
1213.	McCLAIN	James	Final	B. #2 - (1768 - 1776)	325
1214.	MYER	John	Final	B. #2 - (1768 - 1776)	331
1215.	MEDLEY	Eleanor	Account	G.M. #1 - (1777 - 1799)	13
1216.	MEIRS	Jacob	Account	G.M. #1 - (1777 - 1799)	42

1217.	MACKELL	James	Account	G.M. #1 - (1777 - 1799)	45
1218.	MOCKEBOY	Higgonson	Account	G.M. #1 - (1777 - 1799)	57
1219.	MONISS	Jonathan	Final	G.M. #1 - (1777 - 1799)	60
1220.	MIDDAH	John	First	G.M. #1 - (1777 - 1799)	77
1221.	MARSHALL	Paul	Final	G.M. #1 - (1777 - 1799)	99
1222.	MUMS	Jacob	Final	G.M. #1 - (1777 - 1799)	101
1223.	MDRING	John	Final	G.M. #1 - (1777 - 1799)	114
1224.	MARKLE	Conrad	Final	G.M. #1 - (1777 - 1799)	143
1225.	MARSHALL	William	Final	G.M. #1 - (1777 - 1799)	163
1226.	MILLER	Stephen	Final	G.M. #1 - (1777 - 1799)	183
1227.	MICHAEL	Jacob	Final	G.M. #1 - (1777 - 1799)	186
1228.	MILLER	David	Final	G.M. #1 - (1777 - 1799)	196
1229.	MORE	John	Final	G.M. #1 - (1777 - 1799)	200
1230.	MYER	Jacob	Final	G.M. #1 - (1777 - 1799)	201
1231.	MAXWELL	James	Account	G.M. #1 - (1777 - 1799)	260
1232.	MUMMO	Margaret	Final	G.M. #1 - (1777 - 1799)	264
1233.	MYER	Barbara	Final	G.M. #1 - (1777 - 1799)	305
1234.	MYER	John	Final	G.M. #1 - (1777 - 1799)	305
1235.	MYERS	Yost	Final	G.M. #1 - (1777 - 1799)	306
1236.	MURRAY	Joseph	Account	G.M. #1 - (1777 - 1799)	312
1237.	MATHEWS	Margaret	Final	G.M. #1 - (1777 - 1799)	325
1238.	MANAHAN	Thomas	Account	G.M. #1 - (1777 - 1799)	344
1239.	MANAHAN	Thomas	Final	G.M. #1 - (1777 - 1799)	348
1240.	MATTHEWS	John	Account	G.M. #1 - (1777 - 1799)	401
1241.	MANTZ	Casper	Final	G.M. #1 - (1777 - 1799)	428
1242.	MILLER	Christopher	Account	G.M. #1 - (1777 - 1799)	448
1243.	MAHONY	Daniel	Account	G.M. #1 - (1777 - 1799)	480
1244.	MOCH	Valentine	Account	G.M. #1 - (1777 - 1799)	493
1245.	MCGILL	John	Account	G.M. #1 - (1777 - 1799)	494
1246.	MESNER	Peter	Account	G.M. #1 - (1777 - 1799)	504
1247.	MOBBERLY	John	Account	G.M. #1 - (1777 - 1799)	521
1248.	MOCK	Val.	Second	G.M. #1 - (1777 - 1799)	522
1249.	MATHEWS	Daniel	Account	G.M. #1 - (1777 - 1799)	559
1250.	MAJORS	James	Account	G.M. #1 - (1777 - 1799)	588
1251.	MOUNT	Thomas	Account	G.M. #1 - (1777 - 1799)	601
1252.	MAYNARD	Benjamin	Account	G.M. #1 - (1777 - 1799)	621
1253.	MILLER	Martin	Final	G.M. #1 - (1777 - 1799)	632
1254.	MILLER	John	Account	G.M. #1 - (1777 - 1799)	633
1255.	MAHONY	Daniel	Final	G.M. #1 - (1777 - 1799)	648
1256.	MAJORS	James	Second	G.M. #1 - (1777 - 1799)	659
1257.	MAJORS	James	Third	G.M. #1 - (1777 - 1799)	666
1258.	MYERS	Daniel	First	G.M. #2 - (1800 - 1805)	9
1259.	MAYNARD	Nathan	1st & Fl.	G.M. #2 - (1800 - 1805)	10
1260.	MYERS	Daniel	Final	G.M. #2 - (1800 - 1805)	24
1261.	MYERS	Henry	Final	G.M. #2 - (1800 - 1805)	44
1262.	MASTER	Legh	First	G.M. #2 - (1800 - 1805)	56
1263.	MAYNARD	Thomas	Final	G.M. #2 - (1800 - 1805)	86
1264.	MILLER	Philip	Final	G.M. #2 - (1800 - 1805)	90
1265.	MARTIN	Jacob	Final	G.M. #2 - (1800 - 1805)	112
1266.	McDONALD	Margaret	Final	G.M. #2 - (1800 - 1805)	119
1267.	MAYNARD	Nathan	2nd & Fl.	G.M. #2 - (1800 - 1805)	176
1268.	McBRIDE	Daniel	Final	G.M. #2 - (1800 - 1805)	214
1269.	MASTER	Legh	Second	G.M. #2 - (1800 - 1805)	248

#	Surname	Given	Entry	Book/Vol - Years	Page
1270.	MICK	John	1st & Fl.	G.M. #2 - (1800 - 1805)	252
1271.	MAGRUDER	Frazier Geo.	Final	G.M. #2 - (1800 - 1805)	303
1272.	MASTER	Legh	Third	G.M. #2 - (1800 - 1805)	313
1273.	MORT	Mathias	First	G.M. #2 - (1800 - 1805)	317
1274.	MENSOR	Michael Sr.	Final	G.M. #2 - (1800 - 1805)	324
1275.	MATHEWS	John	First	G.M. #2 - (1800 - 1805)	356
1276.	MATHEWS	John	Second	G.M. #2 - (1800 - 1805)	377
1277.	MASTER	Legh	Fourth	G.M. #2 - (1800 - 1805)	379
1278.	McDONALD	Jacob	First	G.M. #2 - (1800 - 1805)	404
1279.	MILLER	Conrad	Final	G.M. #2 - (1800 - 1805)	408
1280.	McAVICKER	Archibald	First	G.M. #2 - (1800 - 1805)	426
1281.	MILLER	Jacob Sr.	Final	G.M. #2 - (1800 - 1805)	428
1282.	McAVICKER	Sarah	Final	G.M. #2 - (1800 - 1805)	456
1283.	MORRISON	James	Final	G.M. #2 - (1800 - 1805)	480
1284.	MATHEWS	John	Final	G.M. #2 - (1800 - 1805)	492
1285.	McNEELY	John	First	G.M. #2 - (1800 - 1805)	493
1286.	McGAREY	John	Final	R.B. #1 - (1806 - 1809)	2
1287.	MEASEL	Frederick	Final	R.B. #1 - (1806 - 1809)	26
1288.	MATHEWS	Chidley	First	R.B. #1 - (1806 - 1809)	65
1289.	McCULLY	Joseph	First	R.B. #1 - (1806 - 1809)	84
1290.	MATHEWS	Chidley	Second	R.B. #1 - (1806 - 1809)	110
1291.	MILLER	John	Final	R.B. #1 - (1806 - 1809)	147
1292.	MILLER	John	Second	R.B. #1 - (1806 - 1809)	149
1293.	McDONALD	Jacob	Second	R.B. #1 - (1806 - 1809)	156
1294.	MILLER	Andrew	Final	R.B. #1 - (1806 - 1809)	216
1295.	McNEELY	John	Second	R.B. #1 - (1806 - 1809)	226
1296.	MICHAEL	Andrew	First	R.B. #1 - (1806 - 1809)	241
1297.	MAYNE	Jno. Alias and Jna White	Final	R.B. #1 - (1806 - 1809)	275
1298.	McDONALD	Jacob	Final	R.B. #1 - (1806 - 1809)	367
1299.	MILLER	George	Final	R.B. #1 - (1806 - 1809)	389
1300.	MARKLE	George	First	R.B. #1 - (1806 - 1809)	414
1301.	MARKLE	George	Final	R.B. #1 - (1806 - 1809)	422
1302.	MUMFORD	Mary	Final	R.B. #1 - (1806 - 1809)	458
1303.	MOBBERLY	Lewis	Final	R.B. #2 - (1809 - 1811)	23
1304.	MICHAEL	Peter	First	R.B. #2 - (1809 - 1811)	31
1305.	McNEELLY	John	Third	R.B. #2 - (1809 - 1811)	60
1306.	MARCHANT	Charles	Final	R.B. #2 - (1809 - 1811)	61
1307.	MARTIN	George	First	R.B. #2 - (1809 - 1811)	68
1308.	MARTZ	Balser	First	R.B. #2 - (1809 - 1811)	100
1309.	McCLAIN	William	First	R.B. #2 - (1809 - 1811)	141
1310.	MILLHOFF	Jacob Philip	First	R.B. #2 - (1809 - 1811)	177
1311.	MICHAEL	Peter	Final	R.B. #2 - (1809 - 1811)	185
1312.	McCLAIN	William	Final	R.B. #2 - (1809 - 1811)	245
1313.	MARTIN	George	First	R.B. #2 - (1809 - 1811)	347
1314.	MAYNARD	Thomas	First	R.B. #2 - (1809 - 1811)	369
1315.	MUSGROVE	Stephen	1st & Fl.	R.B. #2 - (1809 - 1811)	390
1316.	MATHEWS	Chidley	Third	R.B. #2 - (1809 - 1811)	404
1317.	MAYNARD	Thomas	Second	R.B. #2 - (1809 - 1811)	409
1318.	MARTZ	Balser	2nd & Fl.	R.B. #2 - (1809 - 1811)	417
1319.	MICHAEL	Andrew	2nd & Fl.	R.B. #2 - (1809 - 1811)	444
1320.	MARTIN	George	2nd & Fl.	R.B. #2 - (1809 - 1811)	463
1321.	MILLER	Gottlob	Final	R.B. #3 - (1812 - 1815)	2

1322.	MILLHOOFF	Jacob Philip	2nd	R.B. #3 - (1812 - 1815)	63
1323.	MARSHALL	William	First	R.B. #3 - (1812 - 1815)	70
1324.	McWILLIAMS	John	First	R.B. #3 - (1812 - 1815)	141
1325.	MARKLE	Margaret	1st & Fl.	R.B. #3 - (1812 - 1815)	144
1326.	MOCK	Peter	1st & Fl.	R.B. #3 - (1812 - 1815)	147
1327.	MCWILLIAM	John	2nd & Fl.	R.B. #3 - (1812 - 1815)	196
1328.	McCULLY	Robert	1st & Fl.	R.B. #3 - (1812 - 1815)	253
1329.	MAYNARD	Brice	First	R.B. #3 - (1812 - 1815)	268
1330.	McKORKLE	Robert	1st & Fl.	R.B. #3 - (1812 - 1815)	338
1331.	MILLER	Ludwick	1st & Fl.	R.B. #3 - (1812 - 1815)	357
1332.	MILLER	Conrad	First	R.B. #3 - (1812 - 1815)	359
1333.	McDONALD	James	1st & Fl.	R.B. #3 - (1812 - 1815)	365
1334.	MORSELL	William	First	R.B. #3 - (1812 - 1815)	426
1335.	MOYER	Jacob	First	H.S. #1 - (1815 - 1816)	1
1336.	MOYER	Jacob	Second	H.S. #1 - (1815 - 1816)	7
1337.	MOSER	Conrad	1st & Fl.	H.S. #1 - (1815 - 1816)	31
1338.	MILLER	Abraham	First	H.S. #1 - (1815 - 1816)	40
1339.	MAYNARD	Elizabeth	1st & Fl.	H.S. #1 - (1815 - 1816)	41
1340.	MEASEL	Frederick	First	H.S. #1 - (1815 - 1816)	61
1341.	McELFRESH	Sarah	First	H.S. #1 - (1815 - 1816)	71
1342.	MYERS	Peter	First	H.S. #1 - (1815 - 1816)	114
1343.	MARLBOROUGH	Luke	1st & Fl.	H.S. #1 - (1815 - 1816)	124
1344.	MASONHEINER	Peter	First	H.S. #1 - (1815 - 1816)	149
1345.	MILLHOFF	Philip Jacob	Third	H.S. #1 - (1815 - 1816)	159
1346.	McDONALD	James	Final	G.M. #1 - (1777 - 1799)	92
1347.	McLEAN	Alexander	Final	G.M. #1 - (1777 - 1799)	108
1348.	McHARGE	John	Final	G.M. #1 - (1777 - 1799)	138
1349.	McKEEN	James	Final	G.M. #1 - (1777 - 1799)	145
1350.	McHOY	John	Final	G.M. #1 - (1777 - 1799)	153
1351.	McFEE	William	Final	G.M. #1 - (1777 - 1799)	169
1352.	McLAIN	John	Final	G.M. #1 - (1777 - 1799)	185
1353.	McDONALD	Rebekah	Account	G.M. #1 - (1777 - 1799)	274
1354.	McKEEN	William	Account	G.M. #1 - (1777 - 1799)	413
1355.	McKAIN	William	Second	G.M. #1 - (1777 - 1799)	432
1356.	McPHERRIN	Samuel	Account	G.M. #1 - (1777 - 1799)	450
1357.	McPHERRIN	Samuel	Final	G.M. #1 - (1777 - 1799)	471
1358.	McGILL	John	Account	G.M. #1 - (1777 - 1799)	494
1359.	McGILL	John	Second	G.M. #1 - (1777 - 1799)	514
1360.	McILFRESH	John	Account	G.M. #1 - (1777 - 1799)	576
1361.	NICHOLE	William	Account	A. #1 - (1750 - 1767)	31
1362.	NELSON	Arthur	Account	A. #1 - (1750 - 1767)	64
1363.	NEEDHAM	John	Account	A. #1 - (1750 - 1767)	113
1364.	NEEDHAM	John	Addl.	A. #1 - (1750 - 1767)	134
1365.	NORRIS	William	Account	A. #1 - (1750 - 1767)	146
1366.	NELSON	John	Account	A. #1 - (1750 - 1767)	166
1367.	NICHOLE	John	Account	A. #1 - (1750 - 1767)	182
1368.	NORRIS	Samuel	Account	A. #1 - (1750 - 1767)	440
1369.	NORTHCRAFT	Edward	Account	B. #2 - (1768 - 1776)	21
1370.	NELSON	Burgess	Account	B. #2 - (1768 - 1776)	23
1371.	NELSON	Burgess	Final	B. #2 - (1768 - 1776)	60
1372.	NEEDHAM	Jno.	Final	B. #2 - (1768 - 1776)	274
1373.	NORRIS	William	Final	B. #2 - (1768 - 1776)	288
1374.	NEEDHAM	John	Second	B. #2 - (1768 - 1776)	291

1375. NOGLE	George	Final	B. #2 - (1768 - 1776)	381
1376. NORRIS	Benjamin	Account	G.M. #1 - (1777 - 1799)	85
1377. MANTREES	Hardman	Final	G.M. #1 - (1777 - 1799)	120
1378. NEAD	George	Final	G.M. #1 - (1777 - 1799)	129
1379. NORRISS	Thomas	Final	G.M. #1 - (1777 - 1799)	197
1380. NEWMAN	Charles Fredk.	Account	G.M. #1 - (1777 - 1799)	337
1381. NORRIS	Thomas	Final	G.M. #1 - (1777 - 1799)	353
1382. NORWOOD	Richard	Account	G.M. #1 - (1777 - 1799)	430
1383. NULL	Wendell	Final	G.M. #1 - (1777 - 1799)	463
1384. NEALE	Joseph	Final	G.M. #2 - (1800 - 1805)	160
1385. NICODEMUS	Henry	Final	G.M. #2 - (1800 - 1805)	219
1386. NAIL	Daniel Philip	First	R.B. #1 - (1806 - 1809)	6
1387. NAIL	Daniel Philip	Second	R.B. #1 - (1806 - 1809)	160
1388. NOLAND	Thomas Jr.	First	R.B. #2 - (1809 - 1811)	203
1389. NICHOLS	John	First	R.B. #2 - (1809 - 1811)	305
1390. NICHOLS	John	2nd & Fl.	R.B. #3 - (1812 - 1815)	102
1391. NYHOOF	DanieL John	1st & Fl.	R.B. #3 - (1812 - 1815)	167
1392. NORRIS	Nathaniel	First	R.B. #3 - (1812 - 1815)	178
1393. NORRIS	Nathaniel	2nd & Fl.	R.B. #3 - (1812 - 1815)	193
1394. NICODEMUS	Valentine	1st & Fl.	R.B. #3 - (1812 - 1815)	239
1395. NUSS	Michael	1st & Fl.	R.B. #3 - (1812 - 1815)	406
1396. NICODEMUS	Henry	Final	H.S. #1 - (1815 - 1816)	87
1397. NULL	Valentine	1st & Fl.	H.S. #1 - (1815 - 1816)	229
1398. NELSON	Roger	First	H.S. #1 - (1815 - 1816)	254
1399. OFFUTT	James	Account	A. #1 - (1759 - 1767)	43
1400. ODELL	Rignal	Account	A. #1 - (1750 - 1767)	87
1401. OGLE	Joseph	Account	A. #1 - (1750 - 1767)	173
1402. O'NEALL	William	Account	A. #1 - (1750 - 1767)	210
1403. OWENS	Robert	Account	A. #1 - (1750 - 1767)	422
1404. OWEN	Spicer	Account	B. #2 - (1768 - 1776)	38
1405. OFFUTT	James	Final	B. #2 - (1768 - 1776)	82
1406. ODELL	Thomas	Final	B. #2 - (1768 - 1776)	88
1407. OGLE	Joseph	Final	B. #2 - (1768 - 1776)	106
1408. OWLER	George	Final	B. #2 - (1768 - 1776)	124
1409. OWEN	Edward	Account	B. #2 - (1768 - 1776)	149
1410. OWEN	Edward	Addl.	B. #2 - (1768 - 1776)	229
1411. OWEN	Laws.	Final	B. #2 - (1768 - 1776)	236
1412. ORM	John	Account	B. #2 - (1768 - 1776)	251
1413. OFFUTT	Saml.	Account	B. #2 - (1768 - 1776)	266
1414. OWEN	Edward	Account	B. #2 - (1768 - 1776)	356
1415. OFFUTT	Elizabeth	Account	B. #2 - (1768 - 1776)	393
1416. OFFUTT	Elizabeth	Second	B. #2 - (1768 - 1776)	398
1417. ORBISON	William	Account	G.M. #1 - (1777 - 1799)	55
1418. OXX	Adam	Final	G.M. #1 - (1777 - 1799)	136
1419. OGLE	Alexander	First	G.M. #1 - (1777 - 1799)	158
1420. OGLE	Benjamin	Final	G.M. #1 - (1777 - 1799)	172
1421. OGLE	Alexander	Final	G.M. #1 - (1777 - 1799)	177
1422. OWEN	Robert	Account	G.M. #1 - (1777 - 1799)	262
1423. ORNDORPH	Peter	Final	G.M. #1 - (1777 - 1799)	293
1424. OGLE	Thomas	Account	G.M. #1 - (1777 - 1799)	405
1425. OGLE	Thomas	Final	G.M. #1 - (1777 - 1799)	442
1426. OGLE	James	First	G.M. #2 - (1800 - 1805)	114
1427. OGLE	William	Final	G.M. #2 - (1800 - 1805)	118

1428.	OGLE	James	Second	G.M. #2 - (1800 - 1805)	245
1429.	OGLE	James	Third	G.M. #2 - (1800 - 1805)	310
1430.	OGLE	James	Final	G.M. #2 - (1800 - 1805)	363
1431.	ORAM	John	First	R.B. #1 - (1806 - 1809)	114
1432.	ORR	John	Final	R.B. #1 - (1806 - 1809)	119
1433.	OSTERDAY	Christian Sr.	First	R.B. #1 - (1806 - 1809)	179
1434.	OTTO	Peter	First	R.B. #1 - (1806 - 1809)	218
1435.	OSTERDAY	Christian Sr.	Second	R.B. #1 - (1806 - 1809)	318
1436.	OSTERDAY	Christian Sr.	Final	R.B. #1 - (1806 - 1809)	375
1437.	OTTO	William Sr.	Final	R.B. #1 - (1806 - 1809)	394
1438.	ORR	Joseph	First	R.B. #1 - (1806 - 1809)	475
1439.	ORR	Joseph	Second	R.B. #2 - (1809 - 1811)	27
1440.	OSBORN	Daniel	First	R.B. #2 - (1809 - 1811)	45
1441.	ORAM	John	Final	R.B. #2 - (1809 - 1811)	64
1442.	OGLE	Sybilla	Final	R.B. #2 - (1809 - 1811)	201
1443.	OTTO	Peter	Final	R.B. #2 - (1809 - 1811)	207
1444.	OSBORN	Daniel	Second	R.B. #2 - (1809 - 1811)	249
1445.	ORR	Joseph	Third	R.B. #2 - (1809 - 1811)	388
1446.	ORR	Joseph	Fourth	R.B. #2 - (1809 - 1811)	472
1447.	OURAND	Jacob	1st & Fl.	R.B. #3 - (1812 - 1815)	387
1448.	PACK	George	Account	A. #1 - (1750 - 1767)	94
1449.	PRATHER	Josias	Account	A. #1 - (1750 - 1767)	95
1450.	PLUMMER	John	Account	A. #1 - (1750 - 1767)	184
1451.	PEDDYCAART	Nathan	Account	A. #1 - (1750 - 1767)	285
1452.	PLUMMER	William	Account	A. #1 - (1750 - 1767)	298
1453.	PRUITT	Samuel	Account	A. #1 - (1750 - 1767)	363
1454.	PAIN	Thomas	Account	A. #1 - (1750 - 1767)	408
1455.	PELL	Charles	Account	A. #1 - (1750 - 1767)	451
1456.	PLUMMER	Zephaniah	Account	B. #2 - (1768 - 1776)	49
1457.	PELLY	James	Final	B. #2 - (1768 - 1776)	67
1458.	PRITCHETT	William	Final	B. #2 - (1768 - 1776)	84
1459.	PHILSON	William	Final	B. #2 - (1768 - 1776)	122
1460.	PERRINE	John	Final	B. #2 - (1768 - 1776)	156
1461.	PARKS	Joseph	Final	B. #2 - (1768 - 1776)	180
1462.	PERRY	James	Final	B. #2 - (1768 - 1776)	196
1463.	POWLIS	Jacob	Final	B. #2 - (1768 - 1776)	240
1464.	PHILIPS	Philip	Final	B. #2 - (1768 - 1776)	244
1465.	PERRY	James	Final	B. #2 - (1768 - 1776)	254
1466.	PERRY	Rebecca	Final	B. #2 - (1768 - 1776)	257
1467.	PERRY	Benjamin	Final	B. #2 - (1768 - 1776)	271
1468.	PERRY	Rebecca	Final	B. #2 - (1768 - 1776)	315
1469.	PEARL	James	Final	B. #2 - (1768 - 1776)	341
1470.	PEARCE	John	Final	B. #2 - (1768 - 1776)	383
1471.	PRUTSMAN	Lodewick	Account	G.M. #1 - (1777 - 1799)	48
1472.	PENNEBAKER	William	Final	G.M. #1 - (1777 - 1799)	61
1473.	PATTERSON	William	Final	G.M. #1 - (1777 - 1799)	81
1474.	PLUMMER	Samuel	Final	G.M. #1 - (1777 - 1799)	88
1475.	PATTERSON	John	Final	G.M. #1 - (1777 - 1799)	131
1476.	PRICHARD	Jessee	Final	G.M. #1 - (1777 - 1799)	135
1477.	PLUMMEAR	Thomas	Final	G.M. #1 - (1777 - 1799)	183
1478.	PATTON	John	Final	G.M. #1 - (1777 - 1799)	191
1479.	PRATHER	Samuel	Final	G.M. #1 - (1777 - 1799)	192
1480.	PRISH	John	First	G.M. #1 - (1777 - 1799)	259

1481. PERRY	Samuel	Final	G.M. #1 - (1777 - 1799)	279
1482. PRISH	John	Final	G.M. #1 - (1777 - 1799)	284
1483. PENCE	Jacob	Account	G.M. #1 - (1777 - 1799)	309
1484. PLAIN	William	First	G.M. #1 - (1777 - 1799)	351
1485. POWELL	Nathan	Account	G.M. #1 - (1777 - 1799)	380
1486. PATTERSON	Nathaniel	Account	G.M. #1 - (1777 - 1799)	386
1487. PELTZ	John	Final	G.M. #1 - (1777 - 1799)	395
1488. PLUMMER	Sarah	Account	G.M. #1 - (1777 - 1799)	424
1489. POWELL	Nathan	Final	G.M. #1 - (1777 - 1799)	438
1490. PHILPOT	Benjamin	Account	G.M. #1 - (1777 - 1799)	470
1491. PARISH	John	Account	G.M. #1 - (1777 - 1799)	501
1492. PEREGO	Charles	First	G.M. #2 - (1800 - 1805)	57
1493. PHILIPS	Reese	Final	G.M. #2 - (1800 - 1805)	73
1494. PERRY	Sarah	Final	G.M. #2 - (1800 - 1805)	75
1495. PEREGO	Charles	Final	G.M. #2 - (1800 - 1805)	275
1496. PLAIN	David	Final	G.M. #2 - (1800 - 1805)	294
1497. PROTZMAN	Daniel	Final	G.M. #2 - (1800 - 1805)	497
1498. POTT	Benedict	First	R.B. #1 - (1806 - 1809)	253
1499. PRUGH	Conrad	Final	R.B. #1 - (1806 - 1809)	345
1500. PRICE	Thomas	First	R.B. #1 - (1806 - 1809)	447
1501. POOL	Luke	First	R.B. #2 - (1809 - 1811)	13
1502. POTTS	Richard	First	R.B. #2 - (1809 - 1811)	209
1503. PURDY	William	First	R.B. #2 - (1809 - 1811)	246
1504. PUTMAN	John	Final	R.B. #2 - (1809 - 1811)	337
1505. POTTS	Richard	Second	R.B. #2 - (1809 - 1811)	425
1506. PURDY	William	2nd & Fl.	R.B. #3 - (1812 - 1815)	14
1507. POTTS	Richard	Third	R.B. #3 - (1812 - 1815)	36
1508. POTT	Benedict	Final	R.B. #3 - (1812 - 1815)	81
1509. POTTS	Richard	Fourth	R.B. #3 - (1812 - 1815)	156
1510. PATTERSON	John	1st & Fl.	R.B. #3 - (1812 - 1815)	175
1511. PRICE	Thomas	Second	R.B. #3 - (1812 - 1815)	183
1512. POTTS	Richard	Fifth	R.B. #3 - (1812 - 1815)	319
1513. PROTZMAN	John	First	R.B. #3 - (1812 - 1815)	408
1514. PICKET	Charles	First	H.S. #1 - (1815 - 1816)	73
1515. PROTZMAN	John	Second	H.S. #1 - (1815 - 1816)	163
1516. POOLE	Henry Sr.	First	H.S. #1 - (1815 - 1816)	181
1517. POULTNEY	James	1st & Fl.	H.S. #1 - (1815 - 1816)	190
1518. QUYNN	Allen Jr.	First	G.M. #2 - (1800 - 1805)	251
1519. QUAY	Charles	First	R.B. #1 - (1806 - 1809)	317
1520. RIDDLE	Margarett	Account	A. #1 - (1750 - 1767)	4
1521. RAYMAN	William	Account	A. #1 - (1750 - 1767)	68
1522. RICHARDSON	William	Account	A. #1 - (1750 - 1767)	79
1523. RAYMAN	William	Addl.	A. #1 - (1750 - 1767)	143
1524. ROAR	Jacob	Account	A. #1 - (1750 - 1767)	165
1525. RAWLINGS	John	Account	A. #1 - (1750 - 1767)	180
1526. RILEY	James	Account	A. #1 - (1750 - 1767)	202
1527. RADFORD	John	Account	A. #1 - (1750 - 1767)	250
1528. RAY	William	Account	A. #1 - (1750 - 1767)	254
1529. REESLING	John	Account	A. #1 - (1750 - 1767)	288
1530. ROGERS	Samuel	Account	A. #1 - (1750 - 1767)	314
1531. RICHARDSON	Richard	Account	A. #1 - (1750 - 1767)	368
1532. RICHARDSON	Richard	Second	A. #1 - (1750 - 1767)	405
1533. ROGERS	Samuel	Addl.	A. #1 - (1750 - 1767)	418

1534.	RIPLEY	John	Account	A. #1 - (1750 - 1767)	453
1535.	RITCHIE	William	Account	B. #2 - (1768 - 1776)	18
1536.	RICHEY	Henry	Account	B. #2 - (1768 - 17760	96
1537.	RICHARDSON	William	Account	B. #2 - (1768 - 1776)	164
1538.	RAMSEY	Thomas	Account	B. #2 - (1768 - 1776)	211
1539.	ROPP	Nicholas	Account	B. #2 - (1768 - 1776)	215
1540.	RICHARDSON	Mariam	Account	B. #2 - (1768 - 1776)	217
1541.	RECTER	John	Account	B. #2 - (1768 - 1776)	282
1542.	REYNOLDS	James	Account	B. #2 - (1768 - 1776)	371
1543.	RUFE	Darius	Account	G.M. #1 - (1777 - 1799)	1
1544.	RIPLEY	Edward	Account	G.M. #1 - (1777 - 1799)	15
1545.	RIDGELY	William	Account	G.M. #1 - (1777 - 1799)	27
1546.	REIGH	Henry	Final	G.M. #1 - (1777 - 1799)	111
1547.	ROPP	Michael	Final	G.M. #1 - (1777 - 1799)	112
1548.	RIDGELY	Westal	Final	G.M. #1 - (1777 - 1799)	43
1549.	ROU	Valentine	Final	G.M. #1 - (1777 - 1799)	125
1550.	ROTH	Conrod	Final	G.M. #1 - (1777 - 1799)	137
1551.	RICHARDSON	Thomas	Final	G.M. #1 - (1777 - 1799)	181
1552.	RAPE	Valentine	Final	G.M. #1 - (1777 - 1799)	233
1553.	ROSE	Henry	Final	G.M. #1 - (1777 - 1799)	234
1554.	RUNNER	Cutlip	Final	G.M. #1 - (1777 - 1799)	290
1555.	RUSS	Adam	Account	G.M. #1 - (1777 - 1799)	340
1556.	RUSSELL	Josiah	Account	G.M. #1 - (1777 - 1799)	357
1557.	RUSSELL	Josiah	Final	G.M. #1 - (1777 - 1799)	363
1558.	RINEDOLLAR	George	Account	G.M. #1 - (1777 - 1799)	387
1559.	RAMSBURG	Stephen	Final	G.M. #1 - (1777 - 1799)	429
1560.	RAYCOPP	Frederick	Account	G.M. #1 - (1777 - 1799)	439
1561.	RINEDOLLAR	George	Final	G.M. #1 - (1777 - 1799)	447
1562.	RINEHART	Valentine	Account	G.M. #1 - (1777 - 1799)	471
1563.	ROPP	Jacob	Account	G.M. #1 - (1777 - 1799)	497
1564.	RICE	William	Account	G.M. #1 - (1777 - 1799)	538
1565.	ROUSER	Henry	Account	G.M. #1 - (1777 - 1799)	579
1566.	RICHARDSON	John	Account	G.M. #1 - (1777 - 1799)	590
1567.	RAMSBURG	Christian	Account	G.M. #1 - (1777 - 1799)	610
1568.	RENNER	Abraham	Account	G.M. #1 - (1777 - 1799)	640
1569.	RIDINGER	John	Account	G.M. #1 - (1777 - 1799)	649
1570.	RUNNER	John	Final	G.M. #1 - (1777 - 1799)	654
1571.	RINEHART	George	First	G.M. #2 - (1800 - 1805)	137
1572.	RINECKER	Paul	Final	G.M. #2 - (1800 - 1805)	139
1573.	RICHARDS	Caleb	Final	G.M. #2 - (1800 - 1805)	187
1574.	RIDGELY	Richard	First	G.M. #2 - (1800 - 1805)	212
1575.	RICHARDSON	Ann	Final	G.M. #2 - (1800 - 1805)	227
1576.	RUNNER	Michael Jr.	Final	G.M. #2 - (1800 - 1805)	229
1577.	RICE	William	First	G.M. #2 - (1800 - 1805)	235
1578.	RERITT	Alexander	Final	G.M. #2 - (1800 - 1805)	241
1579.	RUDOLPH	Peter	Final	G.M. #2 - (1800 - 1805)	268
1580.	ROBERTS	Richard	Final	G.M. #2 - (1800 - 1805)	295
1581.	RICHARDS	Cathrine	Final	G.M. #2 - (1800 - 1805)	368
1582.	REAM	Balser	Final	G.M. #2 - 91800 - 1805)	388
1583.	RICHARDS	Joseph	Final	G.M. #2 - (1800 - 1805)	437
1584.	RAKER	John	Final	G.M. #2 - (1800 - 1805)	459
1585.	RAMSBURG	George	Final	R.B. #1 - (1806 - 1809)	44
1586.	RUNNER	Michael	First	R.B. #1 - (1806 - 1809)	123

1587. RUSHER	Philip	Final	R.B. #1 - (1806 - 1809)	135
1588. RICHARDSON	Richard	Final	R.B. #1 - (1806 - 1809)	236
1589. RENNER	John	Final	R.B. #1 - (1806 - 1809)	272
1590. ROW	Arthur	First	R.B. #1 - (1806 - 1809)	277
1591. ROOP	David	First	R.B. #1 - (1806 - 1809)	385
1592. RAYCOP	Susanna	Final	R.B. #1 - (1806 - 1809)	397
1593. RAMSBERG	Henry	First	R.B. #1 - (1806 - 1809)	400
1594. REYNOLDS	Hugh	First	R.B. #1 - (1806 - 1809)	416
1595. RUNNER	Michael	Final	R.B. #1 - (1806 - 1809)	435
1596. RICKER	Conrad	First	R.B. #1 - (1806 - 1809)	443
1597. RICHARDSON	John	Second	R.B. #1 - (1806 - 1809)	464
1598. RAMSBURG	Henry	Final	R.B. #1 - (1806 - 1809)	503
1599. RIDER	George	Final	R.B. #2 - (1809 - 1811)	20
1600. RICE	William	Final	R.B. #2 - (1809 - 1811)	34
1601. RUDY	Peter	First	R.B. #2 - (1809 - 1811)	38
1602. RUDY	Peter	Second	R.B. #2 - (1809 - 1811)	57
1603. RICKER	Conrad	Final	R.B. #2 - (1809 - 1811)	80
1604. RICHARDSON	John	Third	R.B. #2 - (1809 - 1811)	90
1605. RENNER	Samuel	Final	R.B. #2 - (1809 - 1811)	102
1606. ROOT	Daniel Sr.	Final	R.B. #2 - 91809 - 1811)	111
1607. RUSHER	John	Third	R.B. #2 - (1809 - 1811)	117
1608. RUSHER	John	Final	R.B. #2 - (1809 - 1811)	167
1609. ROBERTS	John	Final	R.B. #2 - (1809 - 1811)	260
1610. ROBINSON	George	First	R.B. #2 - (1809 - 1811)	281
1611. RAMSBURG	Jacob	First	R.B. #2 - (1809 - 1811)	340
1612. RHODES	Henry Sr.	Final	R.B. #2 - (1809 - 1811)	345
1613. ROBERTS	William Jr.	Final	R.B. #2 - (1809 - 1811)	355
1614. RINEHART	George	First	R.B. #2 - (1809 - 1811)	359
1615. ROOP	David	2nd & Fl.	R.B. #2 - (1809 - 1811)	387
1616. RHODES	Henry Jr.	First	R.B. #2 - (1809 - 1811)	421
1617. ROW	Arthur	2nd & Fl.	R.B. #2 - (1809 - 1811)	485
1618. RUMLER	Davalt	First	R.B. #3 - (1812 - 1815)	29
1619. RIDGELEY	Rebecca	1st & Fl.	R.B. #3 - (1812 - 1815)	100
1620. RUDY	Peter	Final	R.B. #3 - (1812 - 1815)	140
1621. ROOT	Daniel Jr.	Settmt.	R.B. #3 - (1812 - 1815)	179
1622. ROBINSON	George	Second	R.B. #3 - (1812 - 1815)	195
1623. REESE	Adam	1st & Fl.	R.B. #3 - (1812 - 1815)	214
1624. RHODES	Henry Jr.	2nd & Fl.	R.B. #3 - (1812 - 1815)	242
1625. ROBINSON	George	3rd & Fl.	R.B. #3 - (1812 - 1815)	248
1626. REED	James	First	R.B. #3 - (1812 - 1815)	251
1627. RAITT	John	First	R.B. #3 - (1812 - 1815)	257
1628. RUMLER	Devalt	Second	R.B. #3 - (1812 - 1815)	311
1629. ROOT	Elizabeth	First	R.B. #3 - (1812 - 1815)	404
1630. RAITT	John	2nd & Fl.	R.B. #3 - (1812 - 1815)	449
1631. ROOT	Daniel Jr.	First	R.B. #3 - (1812 - 1815)	452
1632. RIDGELEY	Jacob Sr.	First	H.S. #1 - (1815 - 1816)	51
1633. RINEHART	David	2nd & Fl.	H.S. #1 - (1815 - 1816)	146
1634. RIDGELEY	Jacob Sr.	Second	H.S. #1 - (1815 - 1816)	169
1635. STULL	Daniel	Account	A. #1 - (1750 - 1767)	7
1636. SHOUB	Martin	Account	A. #1 - (1750 - 1767)	26
1637. STUDENBAKER	Peter	Account	A. #1 - (1750 - 1767)	44
1638. SCAGGS	Charles	Account	A. #1 - (1750 - 1767)	85
1639. STURRUM	John	Account	A. #1 - (1750 - 1767)	189

1640.	SPRIGG	Edward	Account	A. #1 - (1750 - 1767)	223
1641.	SHUTTER	Henry	Account	A. #1 - (1750 - 1767)	260
1642.	SHAVER	Peter	Account	A. #1 - (1750 - 1767)	267
1643.	STALEY	Jacob	Account	A. #1 - (1750 - 1767)	290
1644.	STALEY	Jacob	Account	A. #1 - (1750 - 1767)	330
1645.	STURRUM	John	Account	A. #1 - (1750 - 1767)	332
1646.	SALTNER	George	Account	A. #1 - (1750 - 1767)	381
1647.	STILLY	Peter	Account	A. #1 - (1750 - 1767)	402
1648.	SELBY	Samuel	Account	A. #1 - (1750 - 1767)	436
1649.	SIDERMAN	Jacob	Account	A. #1 - (1750 - 1767)	456
1650.	SWAN	John	Account	A. #2 - (1768 - 1776)	8
1651.	SELBY	Samuel	Account	B. #2 - (1768 - 1776)	27
1652.	SHELTON	John	Account	B. #2 - (1768 - 1776)	33
1653.	SHINGLETAKER	Jacob	Account	B. #2 - (1768 - 1776)	54
1654.	SAUNDERS	William	Final	B. #2 - (1768 - 1776)	79
1655.	SHEPHERD	John	Account	B. #2 - (1768 - 1776)	94
1656.	STONER	Frederick	Final	B. #2 - (1768 - 1776)	99
1657.	SMITH	Nicholas	Final	B. #2 - (1768 - 1776)	125
1658.	SHEPHERD	John	Final	B. #2 - (1768 - 1776)	130
1659.	SKILES	Elisabeth	Final	B. #2 - (1768 - 1776)	140
1660.	SNAVELY	Leonard	Final	B. #2 - (1768 - 1776)	
1661.	SHOAT	Christian	Final	B. #2 - (1768 - 1776)	176
1662.	SHRIER	Jacob	Final	B. #2 - (1768 - 1776)	182
1663.	SHRIER	Mary	Final	B. #2 - (1768 - 1776)	183
1664.	SPROATSMAN	Laws.	Final	B. #2 - (1768 - 1776)	187
1665.	SMITH	John	Final	B. #2 - 91768 - 1776)	208
1666.	SINN	Henry	Final	B. #2 - (1768 - 1776)	212
1667.	SHIMER	Samuel	Final	B. #2 - (1768 - 1776)	214
1668.	STORP	Peter	Final	B. #2 - (1768 - 1776)	220
1669.	SMITH	Nicholas	Final	B. #2 - (1768 - 1776)	221
1670.	STALLIONS	Richard	Final	B. #2 - (1768 - 1776)	264
1671.	STULL	Adam	Final	B. #2 - (1768 - 1776)	283
1672.	STOCKTON	Robert	Account	B. #2 - (1768 - 1776)	284
1673.	SPARROW	Kensey	Account	B. #2 - (1768 - 1776)	317
1674.	STEPHENSON	William	Account	B. #2 - (1768 - 1776)	347
1675.	SELF	Ann	Account	G.M. #1 - (1777 - 1799)	5
1676.	STEWART	Richard	Account	G.M. #1 - (1777 - 1799)	25
1677.	SPRINGER	Charles	Account	G.M. #1 - (1777 - 1799)	26
1678.	SNOWNBERGER	Jacob	Account	G.M. #1 - (1777 - 1799)	44
1679.	SHUTTER	Christian	Account	G.M. #1 - (1777 - 1799)	52
1680.	SARGEANT	William	Account	G.M. #1 - (1777 - 1799)	56
1681.	STUBBY	Robert	Final	G.M. #1 - (1777 - 1799)	71
1682.	STONER	Henry	Account	G.M. #1 - (1777 - 1799)	71
1683.	SMITH	Rebekah	Final	G.M. #1 - (1777 - 1799)	74
1684.	SMITH.	Casper	Final	G.M. #1 - (1777 - 1799)	79
1685.	SNIDER	Jacob	Account	G.M. #1 - (1777 - 1799)	83
1686.	SWEENEY	Edward	Final	G.M. #1 - (1777 - 1799)	94
1687.	SIMMONDS	Samuel	Final	G.M. #1 - (1777 - 1799)	99
1688.	SHOEMAKER	Peter	First	G.M. #1 - (1777 - 1799)	103
1689.	SHELL	Elizabeth	Final	G.M. #1 - (1777 - 1799)	119
1690.	SNIDER	Sigfrit	Final	G.M. #1 - (1777 - 1799)	123
1691.	SMITH	Jacob	Final	G.M. #1 - (1777 - 1799)	130
1692.	STRYTE	Godfrey	Final	G.M. #1 - (1777 - 1799)	133

1693.	STOVER	Jacob	Final	G.M. #1 - (1777 - 1799)	135
1694.	SCIFER	Felix	Final	G.M. #1 - (1777 - 1799)	142
1695.	SMITH	Charles	Final	G.M. #1 - (1777 - 1799)	143
1696.	SHERFIEG	Casper	Final	G.M. #1 - (1777 - 1799)	146
1697.	SHERTZ	Samuel	Final	G.M. #1 - (1777 - 1799)	152
1698.	SMITH	Mary	Final	G.M. #1 - (1777 - 1799)	156
1699.	SIEGFRIED	CatharIne	Final	G.M. #1 - (1777 - 1799)	158
1700.	STURRUM	Jacob	Final	G.M. #1 - (1777 - 1799)	159
1701.	SLAGLE	Henry	Final	G.M. #1 - (1777 - 1799)	161
1702.	STEEL	Christian	Final	G.M. #1 - (1777 - 1799)	165
1703.	SEARLY	Thomas	Final	G.M. #1 - (1777 - 1799)	167
1704.	SHOAP	Martin	Final	G.M. #1 - (1777 - 1799)	177
1705.	STITELY	Mary	Final	G.M. #1 - (1777 - 1799)	178
1706.	SHOEMAKER	Peter	Final	G.M. #1 - (1777 - 1799)	180
1707.	SOWER	John	First	G.M. #1 - (1777 - 1799)	210
1708.	STORROM	Michael	Final	G.M. #1 - (1777 - 1799)	218
1709.	SIMMONS	Elizabeth	Final	G.M. #1 - (1777 - 1799)	224
1710.	SHEETS	Peter	Final	G.M. #1 - (1777 - 1799)	244
1711.	SUMAN	Peter	Account	G.M. #1 - (1777 - 1799)	246
1712.	SHAFER	Jacob	Final	G.M. #1 - (1777 - 1799)	247
1713.	SHUCH	Peter	Final	G.M. #1 - (1777 - 1799)	253
1714.	SNUKE	John	Final	G.M. #1 - (1777 - 1799)	273
1715.	SMITH	Richard	Second	G.M. #1 - (1777 - 1799)	289
1716.	SMITH	Richard	First	G.M. #1 - (1777 - 1799)	294
1717.	SUEMAN	Peter	Final	G.M. #1 - (1777 - 1799)	303
1718.	STOPPLE	Michael	Account	G.M. #1 - (1777 - 1799)	326
1719.	SMITH	Michael	Account	G.M. #1 - (1777 - 1799)	346
1720.	SCAGGS	William	Final	G.M. #1 - (1777 - 1799)	348
1721.	SMITH	Richard	Third	G.M. #1 - (1777 - 1799)	349
1722.	SMITH	Philip	Final	G.M. #1 - (1777 - 1799)	361
1723.	SWAMLEY	John	Account	G.M. #1 - (1777 - 1799)	368
1724.	STULL	Christian	Account	G.M. #1 - (1777 - 1799)	372
1725.	STULL	Christian	Final	G.M. #1 - (1777 - 1799)	377
1726.	SHOLL	Christian	Account	G.M. #1 - (1777 - 1799)	378
1727.	SPEELMAN	Catharine	Account	G.M. #1 - (1777 - 1799)	385
1728.	SCHLEY	Thomas	Account	G.M. #1 - (1777 - 1799)	400
1729.	SHILLING	William	Account	G.M. #1 - (1777 - 1799)	410
1730.	SNUKE	John	Addl.	G.M. #1 - (1777 - 1799)	422
1731.	SHANER	Peter	Final	G.M. #1 - (1777 - 1799)	437
1732.	SEEPLY	Peter	Final	G.M. #1 - (1777 - 1799)	444
1733.	SHANER	Peter	Final	G.M. #1 - (1777 - 1799)	457
1734.	SWEARINGIN	Van	Account	G.M. #1 - (1777 - 1799)	460
1735.	SHOAP	Christian	First	G.M. #1 - (1777 - 1799)	468
1736.	SMITH	William	Account	G.M. #1 - (1777 - 1799)	477
1737.	SEDGWICK	Josuah	Account	G.M. #1 - (1777 - 1799)	486
1738.	SHAFER	Peter	Account	G.M. #1 - (1777 - 1799)	490
1739.	SIGAFOSE	George	Account	G.M. #1 - (1777 - 1799)	491
1740.	SHRINER	Philip	Account	G.M. #1 - (1777 - 1799)	492
1741.	SHOW	Conrod	Account	G.M. #1 - (1777 - 1799)	499
1742.	SHINGLE	Lawrence	Account	G.M. #1 - (1777 - 1799)	504
1743.	STULL	Adam	Account	G.M. #1 - (1777 - 1799)	519
1744.	SHUP	George	Second	G.M. #1 - (1777 - 1799)	524
1745.	SHANK	Philip	Account	G.M. #1 - (1777 - 1799)	532

1746.	SMITH	Jacob	Final	G.M. #1 - (1777 - 1799)	534
1747.	SMITH	Elizabeth	Final	G.M. #1 - (1777 - 1799)	535
1748.	SMITH	Elizabeth	Final	G.M. #1 - (1777 - 1799)	536
1749.	SHAFER	Henry	Account	G.M. #1 - (1777 - 1799)	548
1750.	STOUP	George	Account	G.M. #1 - (1777 - 1799)	560
1751.	STONER	Benedict	Account	G.M. #1 - (1777 - 1799)	607
1752.	SIGAFOOSE	George	Final	G.M. #1 - (1777 - 1799)	616
1753.	SHOUP	Henry	Account	G.M. #1 - (1777 - 1799)	619
1754.	SHAFFER	Philip I.	Account	G.M. #1 - (1777 - 1799)	622
1755.	SMITH	Richard	4th. & Fl.	G.M. #1 - (1777 - 1799)	644
1756.	SMITH	John	Account	G.M. #1 - (1777 - 1799)	645
1757.	STURRUM	Michael	Addl.	G.M. #1 - (1777 - 1799)	656
1758.	STERLING	Jonathan	Final	G.M. #1 - (1777 - 1799)	657
1759.	SHOTTS	Michael	Account	G.M. #1 - (1777 - 1799)	667
1760.	SAYLOR	Christian	Final	G.M. #1 - (1777 - 1799)	669
1761.	SMITH	Peter	Final	G.M. #2 - (1800 - 1805)	5
1762.	SMITH	Henry	Final	G.M. #2 - (1800 - 1805)	7
1763.	SEDGWICK	Josuah	Final	G.M. #2 - (1800 - 1805)	7
1764.	SPOON	Conrad	Account	G.M. #2 - (1800 - 1805)	26
1765.	SHIELDS	William	Final	G.M. #2 - (1800 - 1805)	36
1766.	SLICK	John Sr.	Account	G.M. #2 - (1800 - 1805)	43
1767.	SIX	Henry	Final	G.M. #2 - (1800 - 1805)	47
1768.	SIMPSON	Sophia	Final	G.M. #2 - (1800 - 1805)	51
1769.	SMELTZER	AdAm	Final	G.M. #2 - (1800 - 1805)	54
1770.	SMITH	Leonard	Final	G.M. #2 - (1800 - 1805)	59
1771.	STONER	Ann	Final	G.M. #2 - (1800 - 1805)	78
1772.	SMITH	Dedrick	Final	G.M. #2 - (1800 - 1805)	89
1773.	SMITH	Christena	Final	G.M. #2 - (1800 - 1805)	115
1774.	STICKELL	Sybilla	Final	G.M. #2 - (1800 - 1805)	149
1775.	STONESIFER	John	First	G.M. #2 - (1800 - 1805)	150
1776.	SIM	William	First	G.M. #2 - (1800 - 1805)	153
1777.	SMOUSE	Henry	Final	G.M. #2 - (1800 - 1805)	167
1778.	SELL	Henry	Final	G.M. #2 - (1800 - 1805)	173
1779.	SIMPSON	Richard Jr.	Final	G.M. #2 - (1800 - 1805)	180
1780.	STONER	John Dr.	Final	G.M. #2 - (1800 - 1805)	183
1781.	STONER	John Sr.	Final	G.M. #2 - (1800 - 1805)	193
1782.	SIMPSON	Richard Jr.	2nd & Fl.	G.M. #2 - (1800 -1805)	196
1783.	STEVENSON	John	First	G.M. #2 - (1800 -1805)	210
1784.	STOUFFER	Daniel	Final	G.M. #2 - (1800 - 1805)	242
1785.	STONESIFER	John	Final	G.M. #2 - (1800 - 1805)	281
1786.	SMITH	Adam	Final	G.M. #2 - (1800 - 18050	305
1787.	SHOEMAKER	Jacob	Final	G.M. #2 - (1800 - 1805)	308
1788.	STONER	George	Final	G.M. #2 - (1800 - 1805)	311
1789.	SHOUP	Christian	Final	G.M. #2 - (1800 - 1805)	326
1790.	STALLINGS	Newman	First	G.M. #2 - (1800 - 1805)	329
1791.	STICKLE	Valentine	Final	G.M. #2 - (1800 - 1805)	332
1792.	STEVENSON	John	Second	G.M. #2 - (1800 - 1805)	342
1793.	STONER	Isaac	First	G.M. #2 - (1800 - 1805)	352
1794.	SNIDER	Jacob Jr.	Final	G.M. #2 - (1800 - 1805)	386
1795.	SPONSALER	Jacob	Final	G.M. #2 - (1800 - 1805)	390
1796.	STALEY	Henry	Final	G.M. #2 - (1800 - 1805)	422
1797.	STONER	Jacob	Final	G.M. #2 - (1800 - 1805)	434
1798.	SHOUP	Christian	2nd & Fl.	G.M. #2 - (1800 - 1805)	440

1799. SHOLL	Cathrine	Final	G.M. #2 - (1800 - 1805)	450
1800. SHROYER	David	Final	G.M. #2 - (1800 - 1805)	464
1801. STRAFER	Yocham	Final	G.M. #2 - (1800 - 1805)	471
1802. SHUEY	Daniel	First	R.B. #1 - (1806 - 1809)	4
1803. STORMS	Isaac	First	R.B. #1 - (1806 - 1809)	40
1804. SINGSTACKS	Philip	First	R.B. #1 - (1806 - 1809)	53
1805. STUDER	Martin	Final	R.B. #1 - (1806 - 1809)	60
1806. SENSENEY	John	First	R.B. #1 - (1806 - 1809)	105
1807. STROWS	Nicholas	Final	R.B. #1 - (1806 - 1809)	134
1808. SHINGLE	Christian	First	R.B. #1 - (1806 - 1809)	142
1809. SLUSSER	Henry	First	R.B. #1 - (1806 - 1809)	143
1810. STONER	Isaac	Second	R.B. #1 - (1806 - 1809)	157
1811. SOMSELL	Devalt	Final	R.B. #1 - (1806 - 1809)	168
1812. STORM	John	First	R.B. #1 - (1806 - 1809)	175
1813. SLATER	Frederick	Final	R.B. #1 - (1806 - 1809)	191
1814. STILLY	Peter	Final	R.B. #1 - (1806 - 1809)	197
1815. STEUART	John	First	R.B. #1 - (1806 - 1809)	211
1816. STORMS	Isaac	Second	R.B. #1 - (1806 - 1809)	242
1817. SMITH	William	First	R.B. #1 - (1806 - 1809)	258
1818. STRAILMAN	Henry	Final	R.B. #1 - (1806 - 1809)	260
1819. STEUART	John	Final	R.B. #1 - (1806 - 1809)	269
1820. STALEY	Henry	First	R.B. #1 - (1806 - 1809)	281
1821. SMITH	William	Final	R.B. #1 - (1806 - 1809)	289
1822. SPONSALER	Andrew	Final	R.B. #1 - (1806 - 1809)	294
1823. SMITH	Sampson	Final `	R.B. #1 - (1806 - 1809)	308
1824. SHIELDS	Jane	First	R.B. #1 - (1806 - 1809)	320
1825. SHEPHERD	John	First	R.B. #1 - (1806 - 1809)	328
1826. SHIELDS	Jane	Second	R.B. #1 - (1806 - 1809)	339
1827. STALLINGS	Newman	Final	R.B. #1 - (1806 - 1809)	356
1828. SLUSSER	Henry	Second	R.B. #1 - (1806 - 1809)	358
1829. STORM	Magdalena	Final	R.B. #1 - (1806 - 1809)	360
1830. SHILKNECHT	Henry	First	R.B. #1 - (1806 - 1809)	368
1831. SHEETS	Jacob	First	R.B. #1 - (1806 - 1809)	433
1832. SALTKELD	Samuel	Final	R.B. #1 - (1806 - 1809)	452
1833. SHUEY	Daniel	Final	R.B. #1 - (1806 - 1809)	457
1834. STARR	John	Final	R.B. #1 - (1806 - 1809)	466
1835. STALEY	Henry	Final	R.B. #1 - (1806 - 1809)	469
1836. STIMMEL	Jacob	First	R.B. #1 - (1806 - 1809)	471
1837. STALEY	Joseph	First	R.B. #1 - (1806 - 1809)	472
1838. STIMMEL	Jacob	Second	R.B. #1 - (1806 - 1809)	484
1839. STORM	John	Second	R.B. #2 - (1809 - 1811)	6
1840. STALEY	Joseph	Final	R.B. #2 - (1809 - 1811)	8
1841. SHILLING	Conrad	Final	R.B. #2 - (1809 - 1811)	62
1842. SAWYEAR	Mathias	Final	R.B. #2 - (1809 - 1811)	98
1843. SINN	Jacob	First	R.B. #2 - (1809 - 1811)	113
1844. SENGSTACK	Philip	Final	R.B. #2 - (1809 - 1811)	123
1845. STIMMELL	Jacob	Third	R.B. #2 - (1809 - 1811)	133
1846. SIM	Anthony	First	R.B. #2 - (1809 - 1811)	136
1847. SIM	Anthony	Final	R.B. #2 - (1809 - 1811)	146
1848. SHILKNECHT	Henry	Second	R.B. #2 - (1809 - 1811)	149
1849. SLICK	John	Final	R.B. #2 - (1809 - 1811)	171
1850. SLICK	Margaret	Final	R.B. #2 - (1809 - 1811)	193
1851. STIMMELL	Jacob	Fourth	R.B. #2 - (1809 - 1811)	247

1852.	STIMMELL	Peter	First	R.B. #2 - (1809 - 1811)	256
1853.	STONER	Isaac	Final	R.B. #2 - (1809 - 1811)	295
1854.	SHEETS	Jacob	Second	R.B. #2 - (1809 - 1811)	312
1855.	SMELTZER	Margaret	Final	R.B. #2 - (1809 - 1811)	316
1856.	SMOUSE	Henry	2nd & Fl.	R.B. #2 - (1809 - 1811)	365
1857.	SHEETS	Jacob	3rd & Fl.	R.B. #2 - (1809 - 1811)	367
1858.	STIMMELL	Peter	Second	R.B. #2 - (1809 - 1811)	395
1859.	STEINER	Jacob Sr.	1st & Fl.	R.B. #2 - (1809 - 1811)	405
1860.	SIDEMAN	Margaret	First	R.B. #2 - (1809 - 1811)	407
1861.	STIMMEL	Peter	Final	R.B. #2 - (1809 - 1811)	410
1862.	STORMS	Isaac	Final	R.B. #2 - (1809 - 1811)	416
1863.	SIDEMAN	Margaret	Final	R.B. #2 - (1809 - 1811)	461
1864.	STIMMELL	Jacob	Final	R.B. #3 - (1812 - 1815)	24
1865.	SLIFER	David	1st & Fl.	R.B. #3 - (1812 - 1815)	47
1866.	STUDAY	Martin	1st & Fl.	R.B. #3 - (1812 - 1815)	54
1867.	SUMMER	John	1st & Fl.	R.B. #3 - (1812 - 1815)	64
1868.	SMELTZER	Leonard	1st & Fl.	R.B. #3 - (1812 - 1815)	79
1869.	SHOVER	George	Final	R.B. #3 - (1812 - 1815)	85
1870.	SMITH	H. John	1st & Fl.	R.B. #3 - (1812 - 1815)	122
1871.	SHIELDS	Jane	Third	R.B. #3 - (1812 - 1815)	132
1872.	SCHLEY	Jacob Geo.	First	R.B. #3 - (1812 - 1815)	133
1873.	SOWERS	Balser	1st & Fl.	R.B. #3 - (1812 - 1815)	136
1874.	SINN	Jacob	2nd & Fl.	R.B. #3 - (1812 - 1815)	163
1875.	SNOUFFER	John	First	R.B. #3 - (1812 - 1815)	184
1876.	SHELMERDINE	Stephen	1st & Fl.	R.B. #3 - (1812 - 1815)	198
1877.	SNOUFFER	John	2nd & Fl.	R.B. #3 - (1812 - 1815)	216
1878.	SIMPSON	Joshua	First	R.B. #3 - (1812 - 1815)	235
1879.	SHOEMAKER	George	1st & Fl.	R.B. #3 - (1812 - 1815)	274
1880.	STORM	Christopher	First	R.B. #3 - (1812 - 1815)	304
1881.	SIMPSON	Thomasin	1st & Fl.	R.B. #3 - (1812 - 1815)	336
1882.	SIMPSON	Joshua	2nd	R.B. #3 - (1812 - 1815)	344
1883.	SLATZER	George	1st & Fl.	R.B. #3 - (1812 - 1815)	349
1884.	STONE	John Sr.	1st & Fl.	R.B. #3 - (1812 - 1815)	351
1885.	SECRIST	George	1st & Fl.	R.B. #3 - (1812 - 1815)	368
1886.	SHEALEY	Andrew	First	R.B. #3 - (1812 - 1815)	381
1887.	SHOVER	Peter	First	R.B. #3 - (1812 - 1815)	397
1888.	SLAYMAKER	William	First	R.B. #3 - (1812 - 1815)	444
1889.	SWIGART	Daniel	First	R.B. #3 - (1812 - 1815)	463
1890.	SHANEBERGER	Michael	1st & Fl.	R.B. #3 - (1812 - 1815)	466
1891.	SHOVER	Peter	Second	H.S. #1 - (1815 - 1816)	54
1892.	STORM	John	3rd & Fl.	H.S. #1 - (1815 - 1816)	67
1893.	SEAR	Mary	1st & Fl.	H.S. #1 - (1815 - 1816)	79
1894.	STEVENS	Jacob	First	H.S. #1 - (1815 - 1816)	101
1895.	STOVER	Philip	First	H.S. #1 - (1815 - 1816)	134
1896.	SHOEMAKER	John	1st & Fl.	H.S. #1 - (1815 - 1816)	139
1897.	SNYDER	Mathias	1st & Fl.	H.S. #1 - (1815 - 1816)	166
1898.	STOUFFER	Christian	First	H.S. #1 - (1815 - 1816)	175
1899.	SHEALEY	Appalonia	1st & Fl.	H.S. #1 - (1815 - 1816)	186
1900.	SHEALEY	Andrew	2nd & Fl.	H.S. #1 - (1815 - 1816)	196
1901.	SHOTS	Margaret	2nd & Fl.	H.S. #1 - (1815 - 1816)	200
1902.	STARR	Tabitha	First	H.S. #1 - (1815 - 1816)	204
1903.	SWIGERT	Daniel	2nd & Fl.	H.S. #1 - (1815 - 1816)	221
1904.	STOVER	Philip	2nd & Fl.	H.S. #1 - (1815 - 1816)	268

1905.	THOMPSON	John	Account	A. #1 - (1750 - 1767)	19
1906.	TURNER	William	Account	A. #1 - (1750 - 1767)	96
1907.	TOMLINSON	Grove	Account	A. #1 - (1750 - 1767)	135
1908.	TOMLINSON	Grove	1st Addl.	A. #1 - (1750 - 1767)	151
1909	TOMLINSON	Grove	2. Addl.	A. #1 - (1750 - 1767)	159
1910.	THOMPSON	William	Account	A. #1 - (1750 - 1767)	256
1911.	TENNELLY	Thomas	Account	A. #1 - (1750 - 1767)	269
1912.	TOMLINSON	Nathl.	Account	A. #1 - (1750 - 1767)	328
1913.	TRAIL	Charles	Account	A. #1 - (1750 - 1767)	341
1914.	TENNELLY	Thomas	Account	A. #1 - (1750 - 1767)	392
1915.	TROXALL	Peter	Account	A. #1 - (1750 - 1767)	419
1916.	THOMAS	Daniel	Account	A. #1 - (1750 - 1767)	442
1917.	TETER	Devalt	Account	B. #2 - (1768 - 1776)	56
1918.	TRUCKS	George	Final	B. #2 - (1768 - 1776)	99
1919.	TOMLINSON	Johannah	Final	B. #2 - (1768 - 1776)	134
1920.	TEDD	Richard	Final	B. #2 - (1768 - 1776)	151
1921.	TANNER	Peter	Final	B. #2 - (1768 - 1776)	170
1922.	THOMAS	Notley	Final	B. #2 - (1768 - 1776)	190
1923.	TRUNDLE	John	Final	B. #2 - (1768 - 1776)	193
1924.	TALBOTT	Elizabeth	Final	B. #2 - (1768 - 1776)	223
1925.	TOUP	Jacob	Final	B. #2 - (1768 - 1776)	304
1926.	TOMS	Henry	Final	B. #2 - (1768 - 1776)	326
1927.	THOMAS	Christian	Account	G.M. #1 - (1777 - 1799)	36
1928.	TUCKER	William	Account	G.M. #1 - (1777 - 1799)	49
1929.	TRUNBULL	George	Final	G.M. #1 - (1777 - 1799)	122
1930.	TRESNER	Jacob	Account	G.M. #1 - (1777 - 1799)	150
1931.	TANEY	Michael	First	G.M. #1 - (1777 - 1799)	190
1932.	TRESNER	Jacob	Final	G.M. #1 - (1777 - 1799)	191
1933.	TANNEHILL	Carlton	First	G.M. #1 - (1777 - 1799)	256
1934.	TEMBLE	George	Final	G.M. #1 - (1777 - 1799)	311
1935.	TAWNEY	Adam	Final	G.M. #1 - (1777 - 1799)	314
1936.	TRINE	Philip	Final	G.M. #1 - (1777 - 1799)	334
1937.	TENER	Henry	Final	G.M. #1 - (1777 - 1799)	354
1938.	TAWNEY	Michael	Account	G.M. #1 - (1777 - 1799)	389
1939.	TROUTMAN	Michael	Final	G.M. #1 - (1777 - 1799)	450
1940.	TROUT	Michael	Final	G.M. #1 - (1777 - 1799)	456
1941.	THOMAS	William	Account	G.M. #1 - (1777 - 1799)	474
1942.	THOMAS	Gabriel	Account	G.M. #1 - (1777 - 1799)	507
1943.	THOMAS	Valentine	Account	G.M. #1 - (1777 - 1799)	597
1944.	THOMAS	John	Account	G.M. #1 - (1777 - 1799)	626
1945.	THOMAS	Christian	Final	G.M. #2 - (1800 - 1805)	49
1946.	TROXALL	Frederick	Final	G.M. #2 - (1800 - 1805)	102
1947.	THOMPSON	Andrew	First	G.M. #2 - (1800 - 1805)	209
1948.	THOMAS	John	Final	G.M. #2 - (1800 - 1805)	221
1949.	TICE	Nicholas	Final	G.M. #2 - (1800 - 1805)	225
1950.	TOOLE	James	Final	G.M. #2 - (1800 - 1805)	257
1951.	TURNER	John	First	G.M. #2 - (1800 - 1805)	319
1952.	TRINE	Susannah	Final	G.M. #2 - (1800 - 1805)	495
1953.	TABLER	Melchor	Final	G.M. #2 - (1800 - 1805)	499
1954.	TAYE	Ferdenand	First	R.B. #1 - (1806 - 1809)	15
1955.	TROXAL	Peter	Final	R.B. #1 - (1806 - 1809)	88
1956.	TAYLOR	Philpot Chas.	Final	R.B. #1 - (1806 - 1809)	107
1957.	THOMAS	John	Final	R.B. #1 - (1806 - 1809)	151

#	Surname	Given Name	Type	Book	Page
1958.	TROUT	Jacob	Final	R.B. #1 - (1806 - 1809)	163
1959.	TAYS	Ferdinand	Final	R.B. #1 - (1806 - 1809)	170
1960.	TABLER	William	First	R.B. #1 - (1806 - 1809)	193
1961.	TABLER	William	Final	R.B. #1 - (1806 - 1809)	264
1962.	THRASHER	Thomas	Final	R.B. #1 - (1806 - 1809)	284
1963.	TOFLER	Peter	1st & Fl.	R.B. #1 - (1806 - 1809)	299
1964.	TROXEL	Magdalena	1st & Fl.	R.B. #1 - (1806 - 1809)	412
1965.	TOBERY	Joshua	First	R.B. #1 - (1806 - 1809)	449
1966.	THOMAS	Peter	1st & Fl.	R.B. #1 - (1806 - 1809)	480
1967.	TOBERRY	Joshua	Final	R.B. #2 - (1809 - 1811)	17
1968.	THOMAS	Gabriel	First	R.B. #2 - (1809 - 1811)	164
1969.	THOMAS	Gabriel	Final	R.B. #2 - (1809 - 1811)	175
1970.	THOMAS	Amos	First	R.B. #2 - (1809 - 1811)	287
1971.	THOMAS	Amos	2nd & Fl.	R.B. #2 - (1809 - 1811)	400
1972.	THOMAS	Rebecca	1st & Fl.	R.B. #2 - (1809 - 1811)	459
1973.	TAYLOR	Joseph	First	R.B. #3 - (1812 - 1815)	97
1974.	TIDY	James	1st & Fl.	H.S. #1 - (1815 - 1816)	97
1975.	TEMPLIN	Samuel	First	H.S. #1 - (1815 - 1816)	199
1976.	UNSELD	Frederick	Account	A. #1 - (1750 - 1767)	175
1977.	UNGLEBERRY	Philip	Final	G.M. #1 - (1777 - 1799)	300
1978.	UMSTEAD	Nicholas	Final	G.M. #1 - (1777 - 1799)	635
1979.	UHLEE	Michael	Final	G.M. #1 - (1777 - 1799)	641
1980.	UMBAUGH	William	Final	R.B. #2 - (1809 - 1811)	115
1981.	VANDIVER	John	Account	A. #1 - (1750 - 1767)	234
1982.	VALENTINE	George	Final	G.M. #1 - (1777 - 1799)	173
1983.	VANTREESE	Hartman	Final	G.M. #1 - (1777 - 1799)	375
1984.	VANHORN	Benjamin	Account	G.M. #1 - (1777 - 1799)	582
1985.	VIAN	John	Final	G.M. #2 - (1800 - 1805)	192
1986.	WARD	Robert	Account	A. #1 - (1750 - 1767)	1
1987.	WOOD	Jacob	Account	A. #1 - (1750 - 1767)	12
1988.	WINDSOR	Notley Benj.	Account	A. #1 - (1750 - 1767)	29
1989.	WALLARICK	George	Account	A. #1 - (1750 - 1767)	29
1990.	WILCOXEN	Roger	Account	A. #1 - (1750 - 1767)	30
1991.	WISE	Francis	Account	A. #1 - (1750 - 1767)	105
1992.	WEST	William	Account	A. #1 - (1750 - 1767)	138
1993.	WILSON	Absolam	Account	A. #1 - (1750 - 1767)	140
1994.	WYVEL	William	Account	A. #1 - (1750 - 1767)	144
1995.	WILSON	Absolam	Addl.	A. #1 - (1750 - 1767)	146
1996.	WILSON	Priscilla	Account	A. #1 - (1750 - 1767)	159
1997.	WILSON	Priscilla	Addl.	A. #1 - (1750 - 1767)	163
1998.	WILLETT	Thomas	Account	A. #1 - (1750 - 1767)	183
1999.	WHITE	John	Account	A. #1 - (1750 - 1767)	213
2000.	WILLIAMS	William	Account	A. #1 - (1750 - 1767)	245
2001.	WILSON	John	Account	A. #1 - (1750 - 1767)	296
2002.	WARFIELD	John	Account	A. #1 - (1750 - 1767)	325
2003.	WOOLHATER	George	Account	A. #1 - (1750 - 1767)	377
2004.	WARFIELD	John	Account	A. #1 - (1750 - 1767)	395
2005.	WELDOR	Saml. Stansby	Account	A. #1 - (1750 - 1767)	412
2006.	WEAVER	John	Account	A. #1 - (1750 - 1767)	416
2007.	WILDS	John	Account	A. #1 - (1750 - 1767)	425
2008.	WILLIAMS	John	Account	B. #2 - (1750 - 1767)	1
2009.	WALLACE	Williams	Account	B. #2 - (1768 - 1776)	36
2010.	WARFIELD	Absolom	Account	B. #2 - (1768 - 1776)	42

2011. WAUGH	Wm.	Account	B. #2 - (1768 - 1776)	51
2012. WALTER	Daniel	Final	B. #2 - (1768 - 1776)	65
2013. WARFIELD	Absolom	Account	B. #2 - (1768 - 1776)	78
2014. WIRTZ	Jacob	Final	B. #2 - (1768 - 1776)	117
2015. WEST	Joseph	Final	B. #2 - (1768 - 1776)	175
2016. WATSON	David	Final	B. #2 - (1768 - 1776)	185
2017. WATTS	Charles	Final	B. #2 - (1768 - 1776)	202
2018. WARFIELD	Absolam	Final	B. #2 - (1767 - 1776)	207
2019. WILLIAMS	William	Final	B. #2 - (1767 - 1776)	233
2020. WILLETT	Edward	Final	B. #2 - (1767 - 1776)	250
2021. WILLIAMS	William	Final	B. #2 - (1767 - 1776)	290
2022. WRIGHT	Joseph	Final	B. #2 - (1767 - 1776)	336
2023. WALKER	George	Final	B. #2 - (1767 - 1776)	369
2024. WILLSON	William	Final	B. #2 - (1767 - 1776)	374
2025. WOLF	John	Final	B. #2 - (1767 - 1776)	379
2026. WILSON	Christr.	Final	B. #2 - (1767 - 1776)	382
2027. WICKHAM	Saml.	Account	B. #2 - (1767 - 1776)	389
2028. WHITENECK	Jno.	Final	B. #2 - (1767 - 1776)	397
2029. WICKHAM	Samuel	First	G.M. #1 - (1777 - 1799)	6
2030. WICKHAM	Samuel	Final	G.M. #1 - (1777 - 1799)	8
2031. WILLSON	John	Account	G.M. #1 - (1777 - 1799)	9
2032. WISE	George	Account	G.M. #1 - (1777 - 1799)	36
2033. WISINGER	Lodowick	Account	G.M. #1 - (1777 - 1799)	48
2034. WAGGONER	Adam	Final	G.M. #1 - (1777 - 1799)	75
2035. WALLACE	Thomas	Final	G.M. #1 - (1777 - 1799)	79
2036. WORTHINGTON	Charles	Final	G.M. #1 - (1777 - 1799)	97
2037. WINHOLTS	Frederick	Final	G.M. #1 - (1777 - 1799)	106
2038. WOOD	Joseph	Final	G.M. #1 - (1777 - 1799)	107
2039. WOLF	Valentine	Final	G.M. #1 - (1777 - 1799)	113
2040. WRIGHT	John	Final	G.M. #1 - (1777 - 1799)	115
2041. WICKHAM	Nathaniel	Final	G.M. #1 - (1777 - 1799)	118
2042. WELTNER	Lodwick	Final	G.M. #1 - (1777 - 1799)	122
2043. WELLER	Philip	Final	G.M. #1 - (1777 - 1799)	129
2044. WELLER	Henry	Final	G.M. #1 - (1777 - 1799)	172
2045. WOOLSEY	George	First	G.M. #1 - (1777 - 1799)	175
2046. WINE	Frederick	Account	G.M. #1 - (1777 - 1799)	203
2047. WHITE	Philip	First	G.M. #1 - (1777 - 1799)	210
2048. WOLF	Adam	Final	G.M. #1 - (1777 - 1799)	213
2049. WITHROW	William	Final	G.M. #1 - (1777 - 1799)	226
2050. WHITE	Philip	Second	G.M. #1 - (1777 - 1799)	230
2051. WINHOLTZ	Conrad	Final	G.M. #1 - (1777 - 1799)	239
2052. WALTZ	Charity	Final	G.M. #1 - (1777 - 1799)	249
2053. WALTZ	Conrad	Final	G.M. #1 - (1777 - 1799)	250
2054. WOLVERTON	Isaac	Final	G.M. #1 - (1777 - 1799)	252
2055. WIGALE	Sebastian	Final	G.M. #1 - (1777 - 1799)	301
2056. WAGGONER	Martin	Final	G.M. #1 - (1777 - 1799)	320
2057. WARNER	George	Final	G.M. #1 - (1777 - 1799)	371
2058. WINHOLTZ	Frederick	Account	G.M. #1 - (1777 - 1799)	384
2059. WINTZ	George	Account	G.M. #1 - (1777 - 1799)	394
2060. WELLER	Philip	Account	G.M. #1 - (1777 - 1799)	399
2061. WARFIELD	Charles	Final	G.M. #1 - (1777 - 1799)	417
2062. WILLSON	William	First	G.M. #1 - (1777 - 1799)	421
2063. WINPEAGLER	George	Account	G.M. #1 - (1777 - 1799)	426

2064.	WEINERT	Mathias	Account	G.M. #1 - (1777 - 1799)	427
2065.	WHIP	Martin	Account	G.M. #1 - (1777 - 1799)	434
2066.	WEINERT	Matthias	Addl. Fl.	G.M. #1 - (1777 - 1799)	457
2067.	WOOD	Joseph	Final	G.M. #1 - (1777 - 1799)	464
2068.	WILLSON	William	Final	G.M. #1 - (1777 - 1799)	467
2069.	WOOLSLAGER	Nicholas	Account	G.M. #1 - (1777 - 1799)	481
2070.	WERNER	George	Addl. Fl.	G.M. #1 - (1777 - 1799)	482
2071.	WOOD	Catharine	Account	G.M. #1 - (1777 - 1799)	498
2072.	WISSINGER	Catharine	Account	G.M. #1 - (1777 - 1799)	498
2073.	WAMPLER	Peter	Account	G.M. #1 - (1777 - 1799)	546
2074.	WATERS	Azel	Account	G.M. #1 - (1777 - 1799)	567
2075.	WOOD	Henry	Account	G.M. #1 - (1777 - 1799)	586
2076.	WOOD	John	Account	G.M. #2 - (1800 - 1805)	14
2077.	WHITCROFT	Edward	Final	G.M. #2 - (1800 - 1805)	61
2078.	WEAVER	Daniel	Final	G.M. #2 - (1800 - 1805)	98
2079.	WEST	Joseph	First	G.M. #2 - (1800 - 1805)	186
2080.	WALKER	James	Final	G.M. #2 - (1800 - 1805)	189
2081.	WERTENBAKER	Adam	Final	G.M. #2 - (1800 - 1805)	273
2082.	WOOLFE	Christopher	Final	G.M. #2 - (1800 - 1805)	365
2083.	WHIP	Tobias	Final	G.M. #2 - (1800 - 1805)	453
2084.	WORMAN	Jacob	Final	G.M. #2 - (1800 - 1805)	472
2085.	WILE	George	Final	G.M. #2 - (1800 - 1805)	479
2086.	WITMORE	Michael	Final	G.M. #2 - (1800 - 1805)	483
2087.	WALTER	John	Final	R.B. #1 - (1806 - 1809)	29
2088.	WALTER	Jacob	First	R.B. #1 - (1806 - 1809)	71
2089.	WOODRING	Philip	First	R.B. #1 - (1806 - 1809)	76
2090.	WOLFE	Henry	Final	R.B. #1 - (1806 - 1809)	108
2091.	WHITE	Joseph	First	R.B. #1 - (1806 - 1809)	115
2092.	WINEGARDNER	Abraham	First	R.B. #1 - (1806 - 1809)	239
2093.	WINEGARDNER	Abraham	Final	R.B. #1 - (1806 - 1809)	306
2094.	WHITE	Joseph	Final	R.B. #1 - (1806 - 1809)	316
2095.	WARMAN	Henry	Final	R.B. #1 - (1806 - 1809)	340
2096.	WEAVER	George	Final	R.B. #1 - (1806 - 1809)	372
2097.	WARFIELD	Absalom	First	R.B. #1 - (1806 - 1809)	352
2098.	WATT	Robert	First	R.B. #1 - (1806 - 1809)	411
2099.	WERENFELTS	Jacob	First	R.B. #1 - (1806 - 1809)	495
2100.	WEDDLE	Peter	First	R.B. #2 - (1809 - 1811)	67
2101.	WEDDLE	Peter	Final	R.B. #2 - (1809 - 1811)	83
2102.	WORMAN	Mary	First	R.B. #2 - (1809 - 1811)	132
2103.	WARFIELD	Absolom	Second	R.B. #2 - (1809 - 1811)	153
2104.	WEDDLE	Leonard	First	R.B. #2 - (1809 - 1811)	182
2105.	WILLIARD	Devalt	Final	R.B. #2 - (1809 - 1811)	195
2106.	WEDDLE	Leonard	Final	R.B. #2 - (1809 - 1811)	199
2107.	WIANT	Yost	First	R.B. #2 - (1809 - 1811)	263
2108.	WORMAN	Mary	Final	R.B. #2 - (1809 - 1811)	274
2109.	WINEMILLER	Henry	First	R.B. #2 - (1809 - 1811)	453
2110.	WINEMILLER	Henry	Second	R.B. #2 - (1809 - 1811)	462
2111.	WARFIELD	Absalom	Third	R.B. #3 - (1812 - 1815)	84
2112.	WORMAN	Andrew	First	R.B. #3 - (1812 - 1815)	104
2113.	WIANT	Yost	2nd & Fl.	R.B. #3 - (1812 - 1815)	124
2114.	WELLER	Jacob	First	R.B. #3 - (1812 - 1815)	170
2115.	WILLIAR	John Sr.	1st & Fl.	R.B. #3 - (1812 - 1815)	172
2116.	WARFIELD	Absalom	4th. & Fl.	R.B. #3 - (1812 - 1815)	212

#	Surname	Given	Entry	Type	Date Range	Page
2117.	WEDDLE	Susanna	1st & Fl.	R.B. #3	(1812 - 1815)	226
2118.	WALTER	Jacob	2nd & Fl.	R.B. #3	(1812 - 1815)	261
2119.	WHITCRAFT	Marcy	First	R.B. #3	(1812 - 1815)	280
2120.	WHITCRAFT	Marcy	2nd & Fl.	R.B. #3	(1812 - 1815)	290
2121.	WORMAN	Andrew	Second	R.B. #3	(1812 - 1815)	303
2122.	WORMAN	Andrew	Third	R.B. #3	(1812 - 1815)	335
2123.	WISE	Joseph	First	R.B. #3	(1812 - 1815)	362
2124.	WITMORE	Abraham	1st & Fl.	R.B. #3	(1812 - 1815)	375
2125.	WARFIELD	Alexander	First	R.B. #3	(1812 - 1815)	378
2126.	WISE	Joseph	Second	R.B. #3	(1812 - 1815)	384
2127.	WILLIS	Henry	First	R.B. #3	(1812 - 1815)	390
2128.	WAGNER	John	1st & Fl.	R.B. #3	(1812 - 1815)	440
2129.	WHITE	Andrew	First	R.B. #3	(1812 - 1815)	450
2130.	WHITE	Andrew	2nd & Fl.	R.B. #3	(1812 - 1815)	456
2131.	WARFIELD	Henry	First	R.B. #3	(1812 - 1815)	457
2132.	WERTENBAKER	Barbara	1st & Fl.	H.S. #1	(1815 - 1816)	3
2133.	WANDLE	Jacob	First	H.S. #1	(1815 - 1816)	75
2134.	WHITE	Sarah	First	H.S. #1	(1815 - 1816)	156
2135.	WELLER	Jacob	2nd & Fl.	H.S. #1	(1815 - 1816)	226
2136.	WARENFELS	Jacob	2nd & Fl.	H.S. #1	(1815 - 1816)	249
2137.	YOHAM	Michael	Account	A. #1	(1750 - 1767)	277
2138.	YON	Yoham	Account	B. #2	(1768 - 1776)	228
2139.	YENGLEN	John	Account	G.M. #1	(1777 - 1799)	66
2140.	YOUNG	John Engle	First	G.M. #1	(1777 - 1799)	120
2141.	YOUNG	John Engle	Final	G.M. #1	(1777 - 1799)	198
2142.	YONTZ	George	Final	G.M. #1	(1777 - 1799)	352
2143.	YONTZ	Catharine	Account	G.M. #1	(1777 - 1799)	489
2144.	YOST	Lodwick	Account	G.M. #1	(1777 - 1799)	511
2145.	YERGER	Henry	Account	G.M. #1	(1777 - 1799)	540
2146.	YOST	Harmon John	Account	G.M. #2	(1800 - 1805)	30
2147.	YOST	Ludwick	Final	G.M. #2	(1800 - 1805)	33
2148.	YOST	Harmon Jno.	Final	G.M. #2	(1800 - 1805)	244
2149.	YINGLING	Margaret	Final	G.M. #2	(1800 - 1805)	279
2150.	YANTIS	Daniel	First	R.B. #1	(1806 - 1809)	82
2151.	YOUNG	Jacob	First	R.B. #1	(1806 - 1809)	112
2152.	YOUNG	Jacob	Final	R.B. #1	(1806 - 1809)	268
2153.	YANTIS	Daniel	Final	R.B. #2	(1809 - 1811)	52
2154.	YOST	John	First	R.B. #2	(1809 - 1811)	278
2155.	YOST	John	Second	R.B. #2	(1809 - 1811)	494
2156.	YOUNG	Hezekiah	First	R.B. #3	(1812 - 1815)	15
2157.	YOUNG	Hezekiah	2nd & Fl.	R.B. #3	(1812 - 1815)	51
2158.	YANTIS	John	First	R.B. #3	(1812 - 1815)	312
2159.	YANTIS	Jacob	1st & Fl.	R.B. #3	(1812 - 1815)	417
2160.	YOST	John	First	H.S. #1	(1815 - 1816)	38
2161.	ZACHARIAS	Daniel	Account	B. #2	(1768 - 1776)	188
2162.	ZADOCK	Frances	Final	G.M. #1	(1777 - 1799)	70
2163.	ZERECH	Antony	Final	G.M. #1	(1777 - 1799)	124
2164.	ZIMMERMAN	George	Account	G.M. #2	(1800 - 1805)	105
2165.	ZIMMERMAN	Benjamin	First	R.B. #2	(1809 - 1811)	73
2166.	ZIMMERMAN	Benjamin	Final	R.B. #2	(1809 - 1811)	104
2167.	ZIMMERMAN	George	2nd & Fl.	R.B. #3	(1812 - 1815)	52
2168.	ZOLMAN	Adam	First	R.B. #3	(1812 - 1815)	373

INDEX

ABBELON, Philip 29
ABERT, John 27
ADAMS, Abraham 35, Christopher 24, Jacob 15, 20, Valentine 19, 22, 23
ADAMSON, John 9,
ADLESPERGER, Francis 31, 34, 36
ALBAUGH, John Senr. 47, 48, 50, Peter 49, William 25, Zachariah 16, 17
ALBRIGHT, John 33
ALEXANDER, Elias 1
ALGIER, Joseph 30
ALLISON, John 38, 39, 46
ALLOX, Margaret 32
AMBROSE, Catherine 40, 42, Christopher 26, Elizabeth 41
ANDERS, Abraham 53, William 14
ANDERSON, John 11
ANDREW, Peter 18
ANDREWS, William 5
ANGELL, Charles 51, 52
ANGLEBERRY, Philip 3
ANSTOLL, George 12
APLER, Everhart 6
APPLE, Peter 13
AREHART, Martin 28
ARNOLD, John 21, Joseph 2
ARTER, Michael 43, 44, 45
ASBESHIT, Rudy 8
ATER, George 37
AULD, Jacob 7
AVEY, Henry 4
AVON, Archd. Revd. 10
BABILON, Barbara 212
BACON, Thomas, Revd. 98
BAER, George Sr. 218
BAKER, Frederick 220, Jacob 110, John 133, Nicholas 83, 84, 91, William 147
BALDWIN, Elijah 256
BALL, Thomas 136
BALSELL, Peter 122
BALTZELL, Daniel 202, 239, Jacob 227, 241
BANDER, Sebold 161
BANKARD, Jacob 150, John 148
BARNARD, Nathaniel 117
BARNES, John 90
BARRICK, Christian 135, Handeal 139, John 126, Peter 114, William 163
BAUMGARNER, Everhart 106
BEAL, Elizabeth 140
BEALL, Alexander 60, 69, 74, Ann 207, Basil 59, Benjamin 88, Charles 151, 158, 244, James 172, Joseph 200, Josiah 101, Magruder Ninian 72, Nathaniel 65, Rachel 221, William 67, 75, 78, 80, 103
BEAN, James 196, 199, 243, 247, Wansley 85
BEARD, John 82, Jonathan 165, 181, Peter 198, 204
BEATTY, Dorothy Mary 253, Edward 76, Edward 62, James 61, John 68, Susannah 63, 107, Thomas 178, William 201, 222, 231
BECK, Lodowick 97
BECKENBAUGH, Casper 149, 156, 164, George 186, 188, 225
BECKER, Christian 171
BECKWITH, George 141, 143
BEEL, David 248
BEGGARLY, George 138
BEGHT, Jacob Jr. 249, 252
BEIGLER, Marks 145
BELL, Peter 210
BELLWOOD, Henry 235, 257, Joseph 255
BENSER, Godlip 175
BERRYER, John 119
BIGGS, John 73
BISHOP, John 264
BITESELL, Henry 168, 169
BLACK, Andrew 157, 160, 193, Catharine 232, 234, Joseph 189, 191, 197, 223
BLACKAMORE, Saml. 113
BLACKBURN, John 170
BLACKMARE, Charles 87
BLAIR, William 132, 134, 162
BLESSING, Jacob 263
BOARD, Jonathan 152
BOBRAAR, Henry 109
BOHRER, Abraham 71
BOMGART, Ludwick 166
BOND, Edward 238, 240
BONHM, Malachia 228
BONSELL, Nicholas 58
BONTLEY, Abner 180
BONTZ, Jacob 96
BOOKER, Bartholomew 174, Honicle 95
BOOKEY, Mathias 177
BOONE, Handeal John 86
BOOSE, Peter 267

BOST, Michael 205, VaLentine 205
BOSTIAN, Andrew 146
BOTTENBERG, Michael 217
BOUCKER, Peter 55
BOUGHER, Jacob 230, 270
BOWER, Christian 192, John 137
BOWERS, John 271, Stephen 250
BOWLUS, Nicholas 206
BOWMAN, Samuel 104
BOYD, John 115
BOYER, Casper 167, 203, Catherine 224, Charlotte 213, Henry 155, Hubartus 195, Melcher 128, Michael 130, Paul 108, Philip 216
BOYERLY, Jacob 254
BRADDOCK, Henry 111
BRADILLER, Emanuel 112
BRADLEY, William 268
BRADNECK, Henry 173
BRANGLE, Christian 182
BRAWNER, Edward 70
BRAYFIELD, Jane 179, Samuel 219
BRAZETON, John 144
BRENGEL, George 266, Jacob 131, Lawrence 187
BRICKER, John 120
BRISCOE, James 54, 57
BROADBECK, Henry 211, Mathias 176
BROOKE, James Jr. 94, James Junr. 100
BROTHER, Henry 185
BROWER, Jacob 208
BROWN, Christopher 258, Daniel 190, George 259, 262, Henry Sr. 236, Jacob 53, James 125
BROWNING, Benjamin 142
BRUCE, Williamson 66
BRUNER, Henry 116
BRUNNER, Elias 129, Jacob Jr. 99, John 18
BRYAN, David 214
DUCHA, Peter 127
BUCKEY, John 209, Mathias 242
BURCKHART, George 215
BURGESS, William 105
BURGETT, Mathias 64
BURKETT, Nathaniel 159
BURKHART, George 237, 251, John 265, 269
BURN, Henry 260
BURNESTON, Joseph 121
BURRELL, Peter 56
BURRIER, Leonard 183, 184, Philip 194

BURTON, Eller William 77, 79, 89, 93
BURY, Edward 124
BUSSARD, Daniel 261, Samuel 123
BUTLER, Peter 81, 92
BUTTMAN, Mary 246
BUTTS, Christian 229, John 245, Ludwick 154
BUXTON, John 102
BUZARD, Jacob 226
CAIN, Ann 386, John 355, William 350
CALEPAUGH, Francis 325
CAMMELL, Leonard 321
CAMPBELL, Hugh 284, James 335, Leonard 339
CARBERY, B. John 377
CARMACK, John 361, William 303
CARN, John 374, Magdalena 434
CARNHART, Henry 290
CARNUFF, Henry 304
CARR, Thomas 359, 362, 366
CARRICK, James 297
CARROLL, Daniel 273
CARTER, John 319
CARTY, Thomas 382, 383
CARVER, Samuel 343, 344
CASE, Simeon 298
CASSOLL, John 310
CASTLE, Thomas 391
CHANEY, Ezekiel 292, Richard 302, William 368, 371, 373, 381, 388, 402, 403, 404
CHAPLINE, Moses 282, 283
CHARLTON, Eleanor 256, 358, John Usher 399
CHEESE, Jacob George 277
CHENOWETH, Thomas 392
CHISHOLME, John 337
CHONOEWTH, Thomas 360
CLABAUGH, Samuel 353, 363
CLABOUGH, Frederick 309
CLAREY, William 406
CLARK, Joseph 293
CLARKE, George 279
CLARY, Benjamin Jr. 413
CLAY, George 330
CLEM, George 299, 326
CLOSE, George 369
COFFEE, Philip 305
COILER, George 306
COLEGATE, John 375, 389, 390, 397
COLEMAN, Cornelius 338
COLLINS, Humphrey 347, Jacob 317
COLP, Nicholas 276

COMP, Peter 357
CONN, Thomas 275, 278, 280, 281
COOK, John 300
COOKES, Jacob 435
COOLEY, James 436, 437
COOMBS, Richard 272
COOMES, Baalis 409, 412, 414, 417
COONCE, Nicholas 295, Peter 307, 318
COONTZ, William 349
COOPER, James 427, 432, 433, Robert 429, 431, William 274
COPER, Mary Ann 294
COPLIN, James 333
CORNALL, Benjamin 387, Smith 296
CORNELL, Benjamin 376
COVER, Earhart 426, 428
CRAFT, Frederick Jr. 380
CRAIG, John 400
CRAMER, Adam 364, 367, 370, Casper 365, George 348, Jacob 291, Peter 423, William 393, 407
CRAPSTER, Abraham 430, Ruliff 351
CRAWL, Christian 311, Henry 312
CRAWMER, George 320, 329
CREAGAR, Christian 288
CREAGER, Adam 422, Casper 287, Conrad 408, Michael 314
CREATON, Elizabeth 421
CREPPS, Jacob 315
CRETIN, James 385, 418
CRIDER, Barbara 324
CRISE, John 424, Joseph 394, 396, 411
CRISER, Adam 346
CRIST, Jacob 334, 345
CROMMETT, Jacob 328
CROMWELL, Joseph 323
CRONE, Conrad 405
CRONICE, John 372
CRONISE, Henry Sr. 439
CROSS, Henry 332
CROUCH, James 308
CROUS, Vendal 301
CROUSE, Jacob 285, 286, 289, John 354
CROWL, Henry 313
CRUISE, Paul 340, 341, 352
CRUM, Amelia 440, Martha 322, William 331, William Sr. 419, 420
CRUMBAUGH, Conrad 395, David 378
CRUMBECKER, Jacob 316
CRYSLER, Peter 398
CUBLENTZ, Philip 379
CUMMIN, James 401
CUMMING, William 342, 425

CURFMAN, Daniel 415, 416, 438, Daniel Jr. 410
CURFFMAN, Daniel 384
CURRANS, William 336
CYFERT, Henry 327
DAMAN, Frederick 531
DANNER, (see TANNER, Peter) 465
DARNALL, John 545, 553, Rachel 544, Thomas 543, William 546, 550
DAVIS, Amos Jr. 539, Ann 459, Benjamin 468, Cornelius 466, Daniel 453, 455, 56, Elias 514, 525, Enoch 471, John 441, Luke 512, Mary 537, 538, Meredith 442, 443, 446, 464, Richard 487, 499, Thomas 444, Vachel 467, 469, Walter 511
DAWSON, Nicholas 524
DEAN, Hezekiah 506, John 488, 490
DEBELLEVUE, St. M. Charles 505
DEBUTTS, Robert 450
DEHOFF, Philip 478
DEHOOF, John 503
DELASHMUTT, Elias 472, Lindsey 484, 494, Trammell 532, 540, 552
DELAUDER, David 457
DELAWTER, Jacob 517, 523, 551
DEMMITT, Henry 548
DENVER, William 473
DERN, Frederick 500, 501, Isaac 491, William 516, 519, 520, 530
DERNER, Andrew 515, Jacob 527
DERR, Martin John 535, Michael Geo. 493, Sebastian 496
DEVENBOUGH, Christopher 480
DEVILBISS, Adam 483, Casper 470, Christian 526, George 474, 475, Geo. Jr. 504, George Jr. 518, Geo. Sr. 502, George Sr. 513, 533, John 498, 549, John H. 542, Margaret 554, Michael 447, 448
DICKSON, James 458
DIFFENDAL, John 536
DILL, Nicholas 476
DINTERMAN, Henry 509
DOFLER, Peter 508
DOLL, George 521, Joseph Jr. 510
DORNER, Andrew 507
DORSEY, A. David 492, Crockett 477, J. Crockett 481, John C. 479, Joshua Edw. 528, 529, William 485, 489, 497
DOUB, George 541
DOUGLASS, Robert 460
DOWDEN, Michael 452

DOWNEY, Robert 451
DOWNWOLF, Ann M. 486
DUCKER, William 462, 463
DUCKETT, Jacob 454
DUDDERER, Jacob 522
DUNN, Margarett 449
DURBIN, Samuel 445
DURST, Henry 495
DUTTEROW, Conrad of Jacob 547
DUVALL, Samuel 534
DYAL, William 461
DYER, Edward 482
EADER, Casper 567
EASON, John 562
EASTERDAY, Christian 586, Martin 572
EBEY, Jacob 599
EBY, Christian 575, 577, 579, Jacob 590
ECKELS, Michael 602
ECKMAN, Eva Elizabeth 568, Jacob 563
EHALT, Elizabeth 578
EICHELBERGER, Henry 603
EILER, Frederick 592
ELDER, Bennett/Bonnit 581, 584, 588, Charles 582, 585, 587, Frances 604, Guy 589, 593
ELLER, Geo. Michael 565
ELLIS, Samuel 605
ELTINGE, Cornelius 555, Rudolph 556, 557, 558
ENGLAND, John 574
ENGLER, Jacob 600
ENGLOS, Peter Sr. 598
ENSEY, Richad 591
ERB, John 583, Peter 564
ERBAUGH, Balser 570, Jacob 571
EVANS, James 596, John 566, 569, Robert 561
EVERHART, Andrew 560, Christopher 559, Peter 594, 597
EVERLY, Adam 573, John 576, 580, Peter 594, 595, 601
FAHS, Abraham 673
FAIR, Charles 633
FALCONER, Gilbert 619
FALKNER, B. John 644
FARIS, Joseph 626
FARTHING, James 643
FASE/FUSS, Philip 612
FERGUSON, Robert 621
FERGUSSON, William 662
FICKLE, Margaret 634, Michael 620
FILLER, Balser 615
FIRMWALT, Lawrence 656

FISHER, Jacob 624
FIVECOAT, Jacob 625
FLECK, Lucas 649, Peter 632
FLEMING, Samuel 617
FOGLE, Andrew 628
FORD, John 616, Samuel 663, 664
FOREMAN, Jacob 654, 668
FORER, Jacob 638, 642,
FORNEY, Nicholas 647
FORTNEY, Catharine 637, Henry 608
FOUT, Baltzer 640, Henry 635, 655, 667, Jacob 660, Peter 618,
FOUTS, Baltis 606, Balzer 623
FOX, Balser 653, Peter 658
FRAZER, Henry 636
FREAM, Thomas 630
FREDERICK, Jacob 639, 641
FREESE, David 631, Michael 672
FREICK, Philip 648
FREY, Enoch 665, 666
FRIDDLE, David 657, 659
FRIEDINGER, Niholas 645
FRIEND, Charles 607, 609, Gabriel 610, 611
FRITSPAW, Christian 627
FROSHOVER, Jacob 629
FRUSHOUR, Adam 661, 674, Jacob 646, 650
FULKERTH, Hyronemus 670
FUNDERBURGH, Walter 669, 671
FUNK, Henry 622
FURNEY, David 613, 614,
FUTTON/FULTON, Robert 651, 652
GAITHER, William 742
GALLA, Peter 762
GALT, James 691
GANTT, Fielder 745, John 731, 735
GARBER, Christian 774, 753, Martin 771
GARDNER, Margaret 741
GARNER, Tobias 709
GARRISON, Frederick 679
GARROT, Barton 743
GARROTT, Barton 734, 738
GARTRELL, Stephen 681
GARTRILL, John 686
GASSAWAY, Benjamin 704, John 677
GATTON, Richard 682, 683
GAUGH, Christopher 756
GAVER, Daniel 723, 728, 729
GEBHART, John Jr. 766, 767
GETTER, Valentine 710
GETTY, Alexander 725
GETTYS, Alexander 736

GETZENDANNER, Adam 694, Baltis 713, Gabriel 688, George 724,
GIANN, Thomas 680
GIBSON, Thomas 760, William 684
GILBERT, Barnard 758, 759, 764, 769, 770, Bernard 772, Henry 708, Jacob 706, Thomas 711, 712,
GILLASPIE, David 676
GILLELAN, John 695, 696
GISERT, Catharine 748
GIST, John 722, 739, 763
GITTINGS, Colmore 765, Erasmus 757
GOOD, Adam 773, George 707, 714, Jacob 698, 702,
GOODENBERGH, Casper 697
GOODMAN, William 749
GOSLING, Ezekiel 685
GRABEL, Peter 768
GRABELL, John 718, 720
GRANMER, Martin 689
GRAVER, Magdelena 737
GREENAMYER, William 744
GREENWELL, Elizabeth 750, 754, Philbert 755, Philip 751, 752
GREENWOOD, Philip 690
GREGG, John 687
GRENAMYER, William 746
GRIFFITH, David 699, 705, 715, William 675
GRIM, Daniel 747
GRIMES, Martin 721, Nicholas 761
GROFF, John 716
GROONAMYOR, William 727
GROSH, Conrad 719, Michael 700
GROSHON, Elias 730, 732
GROSHONG, Elias 717
GROSSNICKLE, John 692, Peter 703
GROVE, Jacob 701, Martin 740, Valentine 678
GROWER, Varney 726
GUINN, John 693
HADMAN, Joseph 796
HAFF, Abraham Jr. 945, 946, 958
HAGAN, Hugh 887, 892, 932, 933
HAGAR, David 802, John 833
HAGER, Alexander 829
HAINES, Daniel 806
HALL, Benjamin 939, Edward 837, 849, 850, Francis 938, James 921, Joseph 68
HALLIDAY, James 844
HAMILTON, John 934
HAMMER, Andrew 848, Francis 889
HAMMETT, Robert 856A
HAMMOND, John 923, 930, 950, Thomas 841
HANE, Jacob 866
HANN, Henry 935, Ludwick 948
HARBAUGH, Ludwick 937
HARDESTY, George 834
HARDIN, John 777
HARDING, Charles 899, Elizabeth 812, Philip 838
HARDMAN, Cathrine 813, Henry 865, Joseph 796, Michael 810
HARGARADER, Mary 854
HARGARIDER, Jno. 818
HARGATE, Peter 940, 949
HARLIN, George 788
HARLON, John 846
HARMAN, Michael 790
HARMON, Marks 900
HARPE, John 867
HARPER, Josiah 804
HARRIS, George 903, Rachel 785, Thomas 814
HART, Adam 893, Valentine 845
HARTLAND, George 786
HARTSOCK, Henry 927
HARTSOKE, Margaret 831, Peter 832,
HAUBERT, Elizabeth 959, Mary Eve 960
HAUER, Nicholas 922, 936
HAUN, George 807
HAUSER, Hennick 884
HAVERLY, Michael 859
HAWK, Peter 931
HAWKINS, John 817
HAWN, Leonard 898, 902, Michael 843, 851, 855, 871, 895
HAYES, Zachariah 808
HAYMOND, John 778, Nicholas 809
HAYSE, Jonathan 860, 862, 874
HEARSE, Coonrod 820
HECK, Balser 872A
HEDGE, William 828
HEDGES, Charles 872, Joseph 779, Moses 825, Peter 856
HEFFNER, Fred. Jacob 928, Jacob Fredk. 951
HEFNER, Michael 805
HELM, Francis N. 870
HEMP, Nicholas 823
HERD, Jacob 891
HERRING, Ludwick 947, 952
HERSHBERGER, Bernard 882, Henry 925, 926

HICKMAN, David 819, Henry 791, Joshua 815, Joshua Jr. 803, William 798
HIGDON, John 890
HIGGINBOTHAM, Charles 783, 784
HILDEBRAND, Nicholas 842
HILDEBRICK, George 909
HILDERBRAND, Jacob 917, 941
HILL, Abraham 878, 944, Joseph 888, 911, Margaret 904, 905, Robert 869, Zephaniah 924
HILLEARY, Ann 954, 957, Thomas 929
HILTEBRAND, Adam 801, John 794
HINER, Herbert 907, 912
HINKERLY, Frederick 826
HITESHEW, Jacob 894, Nicholas 916, 919, William 953, 956
HOBBS, John 879, Nicholas 877, 881
HOCKENSMITH, George 880
HOCKMAN, Abraham 852, Jacob 874
HOFFIN, Elizabeth 830
HOILE, John 799
HOLLAND, James 782, Richard 864
HOLLAR, George 886
HOLMES, William 789
HOLTS, Benedict 861
HOLTZAPPLE, Mary 910
HOMES, Thomas 913, 914
HOOPER, Abraham 920
HOOVER, Christian 915, Nicholas 835
HORINE, Tobias 816, 839, 840
HOSPLOHORN, Ludwick 901
HOUPMAN, Tetrick John 885
HOUSE, George Jr. 942, John 780
HOWARD, Cornelius 853, 896, George 897, Joseph 906, 955
HOWELL, Stephen 918
HOY, Nicholas 876
HUFFMAN, Peter 824
HUFFORD, Christian 847, Philip 863, 875
HUFMAN, Jacob 795, John 800
HUFNAGLE, Valentine 793
HUGHES, Jesse 961
HUMBERT, William 836
HUMMELL, John 827
HUMMER, Jacob 822
HUNT, Henry 792
HUNTER, Saml. Rev. 797, Samuel 787
HUSSEY, John 776
HUSTON, Thomas 943
HUTCHCRAFT, Thomas 811
HUTSELL, George 821

HYATT, Seth 781
HYDE, Jonathan 908
HYETT, Seth 775
HYFIELD, Jonathan 857, 858
HYNER, William 883
IJAMS, Plummer 963, 964, Richard 966, 967
ILGNER, Christian 962
ISENBURGH, Gabriel 965
JACKS, John 968
JACOB, Daniel 989
JACOBS, Benjamin 990, George 988
JAMISON, Henry 995, 996, 999, 1002, 1003, 1004, John 997, 998, 1005
JENINGS, John 993, Richard 986
JENKINS, Josiah 972, 993
JESSERANG, Bartholomew 973
JEWELL, George 975
JOHNSON, Baker 1007, Edward 971, J. Thomas 1008, James 974, John 970, 980, 1006, Joseph 982, 1001,Thomas 979, 981, 1000, Thos. 976, William 1009
JOLLAGH, Frederick 983
JONES, John 969, Josias 977, Thomas 978
JUDA, Jacob 991, Philip 992, 994,
JUSTICE, John 984, 985, 987
KARN, Frederick 1066, 1067, Magdalena 1092
KAYCOP, Frederick 1042
KEEFER, Frederick 1062, Ludwick 1076, Margaret 1084
KEEN, Henry 1012
KEEVER, Andrew 1077
KEIN, Joseph 1030
KELLER, Abraham 1017, Barbara 1060, George 1055, 1057, Jacob 1016, 1059, Jacob Jr. 1063, John 1091, Philip 1073, Philip John 1085, 1086, Rudolph 1019, 1022, 1023, 1040
KELLY, Samuel 1010
KELP, Philip 1028
KEMP, David 1045, Henry 1049, 1054, Jacob 1039, John 1015, 1052, 1056, Ludwick 1061, 1064, Nicholas 1027, Peter 1078, 1080, 1082, Peter Sr. 1074, Philip 1075
KENSLER, Jacob 1034
KEPHART, Simon 1058, Solomon 1065, 1068, 1090,
KEPLER, Jacob 1048
KEPLINGER, George 1014
KERN, Jacob 1011, Michael 1033

KERR, Agness 1050, Hugh 1043
KESSLER, Jacob 1032, Mathew 1088
KETULDY, Conrod 1026
KIBLER, Michael 1041
KILE, Adam 1035, Elizabeth 1036
KIMBERLIN, Mathias 1018
KIMBOL, John 1020, Lettice 1021
KING, Abraham 1031, Andrew 1038, Philip 1025
KINKERLY, Frederick 1089
KINLEY, Jacob 1093
KIPPS, Abraham 1037,
KIRTZ, George 1072
KITTAMAN, George 1047
KITTS, George 1013
KITZMILLER, Elizabeth 1081
KNIGHT, William 1046
KNOUF, Jacob 1053, 1071, 1094, John 1095
KNOUFF, Margaret 1029
KNOX, John 1083, 1087
KOELER, Jacob 1044
KOONS, Paul 1096
KOONTZ, Henry 1051
KREGLOE, Elizabeth 1069, 1070,
KRISE, Henry 1079
KUNU/KUNCE, Philip 1024
LABO, Abraham 1126
LAKIN, Abraham 1137, 1148
LAMAR, John 1145
LAMBERT, Baker 1122, John 1175
LAMBKEY, Wm. Christian 1132, 1154, 1162
LANEY, Mathew 1109
LAWRENCE, John 1120, 1121, Martha 1136, Richard 1144, 1164, 1169, 1176
LAYMAN, Christopher 1101, John 1125, Philip Jacob 1118
LEACH, Edward 1180, 1184
LEAPLEY, Peter 1152
LEATHER, John 1173
LEESE, Conrod 1131, Philip 1119
LEFAVER, Christian 1134, Elias 1143, 1146
LEISTER, Nicholas 1149
LEMAR, B. William 1179, Thomas 1097
LESHORN, Paul 1138
LETT, Daniel 1170
LEVY, David Jr. 1158, 1163, David Sr. 1157, 1161, 1167, 1185, Jacob 1171, 1181, Samuel 1186, Valentine 1182,
LEWIS, Thomas 1140
LICKLIDER, Conrod 1115

LIGHT, Philip/Peter 1107
LIGHTER, Melchor 1108
LIGHTY, Jacob 1110
LINEBAUGH, Frederick 1123, 1124,
LINGANFELTER, Valentine 1165
LINGENFELTER, John 1112
LINTON, William 1141, Zachariah 1147, 1168,
LITTLE, John 1106, 1113, Peter 1111
LITTON, Caleb 1102
LIVERS, Henry 1139, 1142, Robert 1128, 1130, William 1166
LOFLIN, Richard 1105
LOHR, John 1117
LOHRA, John 1174
LONG, Christopher 1177, 1183, 1187, Conrad 1172, David 1099, Frederick 1153, John 1155, Ludwick 1150, Mary 1178, Thomas 1114,
LOOKENPEEL, Jacob 1156
LOVELESS, Baptist John 1103
LOW, Andrew 1135
LOY, George 1100, Jacob 1104
LUCKETT, John 1127
LUTZ, George 1129
LYLES, William 1133, 1151, 1159, 1160
LYNCH, Mary 1188
LYNHAM, Bartholomew 1098
LYNN, David 1116
MACKALL, Benjamin 1210
MACKATEE, William 1211
MACKELL, James 1217
MAGRUDER, Alexander 1197, Frazier Geo. 1271, Ninian 1193, 1194,
MAHONY. Daniel 1243, 1255
MAJORS, James 1250, 1256, 1257
MANAHAN, Thomas 1238, 1239
MANTREES, Hardman 1377
MANTZ, Casper 1241, Peter 1198, 1199
MARCHANT, Charles 1306
MARKLAND, Margarett 1192
MARKLE, Conrad 1224, George 1300, 1301, Margaret 1325
MARLBOROUGH, Luke 1343
MARSHALL, Paul 1221, William 1225, 1323,
MARTIN, George 1307, 1313, 1320, Jacob 1265,
MARTZ, Balser 1308, 1318
MASONHEINER, Peter 1344
MASTER, Legh 1262, 1269, 1272, 1277
MASTERS, Robert 1208
MATHEWS, Chidley 1201, 1288, 1290,

1316, Daniel 1249, Edward 1204, John 1275, 1276, 1284, Jno. 1206, Margaret 1237, Samuel 1212,
MATTHEWS, John 1240
MAXWELL, James 1231
MAYNARD, Benjamin 1252, Brice 1329, Elizabeth 1339, Nathan 1259, 1267, Thomas 1263, 1314, 1317
MAYNE, Jon Alias Jna White 1297
McAVICKER, Archibald 1280, Sarah 1282
McBRIDE, Daniel 1268
McCLAIN, James 1213, William 1309, 1312
McCULLY, Joseph 1289, Robert 1328,
McDONALD, Jacob 1278, 1293, 1298, James 1333, 1346, Margaret 1266, Rebekah 1353,
McELFRESH, Sarah 1341
McFEE, William 1351
McGAREY, John 1286
McGILL, John 1245, 1358, 1359
McHARGE, John 1348
McHOY, John 1350
McILFRESH, John 1360
McKAIN, William 1355
McKEEN, James 1349, William 1354
McKORKLE, Robert 1330
McLAIN, John 1352
McLEAN, Alexander 1347
McNEELLY, John 1305
McNEELY, John 1285, 1295
McPHERRIN, Samuel 1356, 1357
McSWAIN, George 1202
McWILLIAM, John 1327
McWILLIAMS, John 1324
MDRING, John 1223
MEASEL, Frederick 1287, 1340
MEDLEY, Eleanor 1215
MEIRS, Jacob 1216
MELOTT, Theodore 1189
MENSOR, Michael Sr. 1274
MESNER, Peter 1246, 1311
MEYRICK, Richard 1203
MICHAEL, Andrew 1296, 1319, Jacob 1227, Peter 1304, 1311
MICK, John 1270
MIDDAH, John 1220
MILES, Thos. 1205
MILLER, Abraham 1195, 1338, Andrew 1294, Christopher 1242, Conrad 1279, 1332, David 1228, George 1299, Gottlob 1321, Jacob Sr. 1281, John

1254, 1291, 1292, Ludwick 1331, Martin 1253, Philip 1264, Stephen 1226,
MILLHOFF, Jacob Philip 1310, Philip Jacob 1345
MILLHOOFF, Jacob Philip 1322
MILLHOUSE, Morris 1196
MOBBERLY, John 1247, Lewis 1303
MOCH, Valentine 1244
MOCK, Peter 1326, Val. 1248
MOCKBEE, Lucy 1207
MOCKEBOY, Higgonson 1218
MONG, Godfrey 1190, 1191
MONISS, Jonathan 1219
MORE, John 1229
MORRISON, James 1283
MORSELL, William 1334
MORT, Mathias 1273
MOSER, Conrad 1337
MOUNT, Thomas 1251
MOYER, Jacob 1335, 1336
MULLENDORE, Jacob 1209
MUMFORD, Mary 1302
MUMMO, Margaret 1232
MUMS, Jacob 1222
MURRAY, Joseph 1236
MUSGROVE, Stephen 1315
MUSSELMAN, Mathias 1200
MYER, Barbara 1233, Jacob 1230, John 1214, 1234
MYERS, Daniel 1258, 1260, Henry 1261, Peter 1342, Yost 1235
NAIL, Daniel Philip 1386, 1387
NEAD, George 1378
NEALE, Joseph 1384
NEEDHAM, Jno. 1372, John 1363, 1364, 1374
NELSON, Arthur 1362, Burgess 1370, 1371, John 1366, Roger 1398
NEWMAN, Charles Fredk. 1380
NICHOLS, John 1367, 1389, 1390, William 361
NICODEMUS, Henry 1385, 1396, Valentine 1394
NOGLE, George 1375
NOLAND, Thomas Jr. 1388
NORRIS, Benjamin 1376, Nathaniel 1392, 1393, Samuel 1368, Thomas 1381, William 1365, 1373
NORRISS, Thomas 1379
NORTHCRAFT, Edward 1369
NORWOOD, Richard 1382
NULL, Valentine 1397, Wendell 1383

NUSZ, Michael 1395
NYHOOF, Daniel John 1391
ODELL, Rignal 1400, Thomas 1406
OFFUTT, Elizabeth 1415, 1416, James 1399, 1405, Saml. 1413,
OGLE, Alexander 1419, 1421, Benjamin 1420, James 1426, 1428, 1429, 1430, Joseph 1401, 1407, Sybilla 1442, Thomas 1424, 1425, William 1427
ORAM, John 1431, 1441
ORBISON, William 1417
ORM, John 1412
ORNDORPH, Peter 1423
ORR, John 1432, Joseph 1438, 1439, 1445, 1446
OSBORN, Daniel 1440, 1444
OSTERDAY, Christian Sr. 1433, 1435, 1436
OTTO, Peter 1434, 1443, William Sr. 1437
OURAND, Jacob 1447
OWEN, Edward 1409, 1410, 1414, Laws. 1411, Robert 1422, Spicer 1404
OWENS, Robert 1403
OWLER, George 1408
OXX, Adam 1418
O'NEALL, William 1402
PACK, George 1448
PAIN, Thomas 1454
PARISH, John 1491
PARKS, Joseph 1461
PATTERSON, John 1475, 1510, Nathaniel 1486, William 1473
PATTON, John 1478
PEARCE, John 1470
PEARL, James 1469
PEDDYCAART, Nathan 1451
PELL, Charles 1455
PELLY, James 1457
PELTZ, John 1487
PENCE, Jacob 1483
PENNEBAKER, William 1472
PEREGO, Charles 1492, 1495
PERRINS, John 1460
PERRY, Benjamin 1467, James 1462, 1465, Rebecca 1466, 1468, Samuel 1481, Sarah 1494
PHILIPS, Philip 1464, Reese 1493
PHILPOT, Benjamin 1490
PHILSON, William 1459
PICKET, Charles 1514
PLAIN, David 1496, William 1484
PLUMMEAR, Thomas 1477

PLUMMER, John 1450, Samuel 1474, Sarah 1488, William 1452, Zephaniah 1456
POOL, Luke 1501
POOLE, Henry Sr. 1516
POTT, Benedict 1498, 1508
POTTS, Richard 1502, 1505, 1507, 1509, 1512
POULTNEY, James 1517
POWELL, Nathan 1485, 1489
POWLIS, Jacob 1463
PRATHER, Josias 1449, Samuel 1479
PRICE, Thomas 1500, 1511
PRICHARD, Jessee 1476
PRISH, John 1480, 1482
PRITCHETT, William 1458
PROTZMAN, Daniel 1497, John 1513, 1515
PRUGH, Conrad 1499
PRUITT, Samuel 1453
PRUTSMAN, Lodewick 1471
PURDY, William 1503, 1506
PUTMAN, John 1504
QUAY, Charles 1519
QUYNN, Allen Jr. 1518
RADFORD, John 1527
RAITT, John 1627, 1630
RAKER, John 1584
RAMSBERG, Christian 1567, George 1585, Henry 1593, 1598, Jacob 1611, Stephen 1559
RAMSEY, Thomas 1538
RAPE, Valentine 1552
RAWLINGS, John 1525
RAY, William 1528
RAYCOP, Susanna 1592
RAYCOPP, Frederick 1560
RAYMAN, William 1521, 1523
REAM, Balser 1582
RECTER, John 1541
REED, James 1626
REESE, Adam 1623
REESLING, John 1529
REIGH, Henry 1546
RENNER, Abraham 1568, John 1589, Samuel 1605
RERITT, Alexander 1578
REYNOLDS, Hugh 1594, James 1542
RHODES, Henry Sr. 1612, Henry Jr. 1616, 1624
RICE, William 1564, 1577, 1600
RICHARDS, Caleb 1573, Cathrine 1581, Joseph 1583,

RICHARDSON, Ann 1575, John 1566, 1597, 1604, Mariam 1540, Richard 1531, 1532, 1588, Thomas 1551, William 1522, 1537
RICHEY, Henry 1536
RICKER, Conrad 1596, 1603,
RIDDLE, Margarett 1520
RIDER, George 1599
RIDGELEY, Jacob Sr. 1632, 1634, Rebecca 1619
RIDGELY, Richard 1574, Westal 1548, William 1545
RIDINGER, John 1569
RILEY, James 1526
RINECKER, Paul 1572
RINEDOLLAR, George 1558, 1561
RINEHART, David 1633, George 1571, 1614, Valentine 1562
RIPLEY, Edward 1544, John 1534,
RITCHIE, William 1535
ROAR, Jacob 1524
ROBERTS, John 1609, Richard 1580, William Jr. 1613
ROBINSON, George 1610, 1622, 1625
ROGERS, Samuel 1530, 1533
ROOP, David 1591, 1615
ROOT, Daniel Jr. 1621, 1631, Daniel Sr. 1606, Elizabeth 1629
ROPP, Jacob 1563, Michael 1547, Nicholas 1539
ROSE, Henry 1553
ROTH, Conrod 1550
ROU, Valentine 1549
ROUSER, Henry 1565
ROW, Arthur 1590, 1617
RUDOLPH, Peter 1579
RUDY, Peter 1601, 1602, 1620
RUFE, Darius 1543
RUMLER, Davalt 1618, 1628
RUNNER, Cutlip 1554, John 1570, Michael 1586, 1595, Michael Jr. 1576
RUSHER, John 1607, 1608, Philip 1587
RUSS, Adam 1555
RUSSELL, Josiah 1556, 1557
SALTKELD, Samuel 1832
SALTNER, George 1646
SARGEANT, William 1680
SAUNDERS, William 1654
SAWYEAR, Mathias 1842
SAYLOR, Christian 1760
SCAGGS, Charles 1638, William 1720
SCHLEY, Jacob Geo. 1872, Thomas 1728
SCIFER, Felix 1694

SEAR, Mary 1893
SEARLY, Thomas 1703
SECRIST, George 1885
SEDGWICK, Josuah 1737, 1763
SEEPLY, Peter 1732
SELBY, Samuel 1648, 1651
SELF, Ann 1675
SELL, Henry 1778
SENGSTACK, Philip 1844
SENSENEY, John 1806
SHAFER, Henry 1749, Jacob 1712, Peter 1738
SHAFFER, Philip I. 1754
SHANEBERGER, Michael 1890
SHANER, Peter 1731, 1733
SHANK, Philip 1745
SHAVER, Peter 1642
SHEALEY, Andrew 1886, 1900, Appalonia 899
SHEETS, Jacob 1831, 1854, 1857, Peter 1710
SHELL, Elizabeth 1689
SHELMERDINE, Stephen 1876
SHELTON, John 1652
SHEPHERD, John 1655, 1658, 1825
SHERFIEG, Casper 1696
SHERTZ, Samuel 1697
SHIELDS, Jane 1824, 1826, 1871, William 1765
SHILKNECHT, Henry 1830, 1848
SHILLING, Conrad 1841, William 1729
SHIMER, Samuel 1667
SHINGLE, Christian 1808, Lawrence 1742
SHINGLETAKER, Jacob 1653
SHOAP, Christian 1735, Martin 1704
SHOAT, Christian 1661
SHOEMAKER, George 1879, Jacob 1787, John 1896, Peter 1688, 1706
SHOLL, Cathrine 1799, Christian 1726
SHOTS, Margaret 1901
SHOTTS, Michael 1759
SHOUB, Martin 1636
SHOUP, Christian 1789, 1798, Henry 1753
SHOVER, George 1869, Peter 1887, 1891
SHOW, Conrod 1741
SHRIER, Jacob 1662, Mary 1663
SHRINER, Phillp 1740
SHROYER, David 1800
SHUCH, Peter 1713
SHUEY, Daniel 1802, 1833

SHUP, George 1744
SHUTTER, Christian 1679, Henry 1641
SIDEMAN, Margaret 1860, 1863
SIDERMAN, Jacob 1649
SIEGFRIED, Catharine 1699
SIGAFOOSE, George 1752
SIGAFOSE, George 1739
SIM, Anthony 1846, 1847, William 1776
SIMMONDS, Samuel 1687
SIMMONS, Elizabeth 1709
SIMPSON, Joshua 1878, 1882, Richard Jr. 1779, 1782, Sophia 1768, Thomasin 1881
SINGSTACKS, Philip 1804
SINN, Henry 1666, Jacob 1843, 1874
SIX, Henry 1767
SKILES, Elisabeth 1659
SLAGLE, Henry 1701
SLATER, Frederick 1813
SLATZER, George 1883
SLAYMAKER, William 1888
SLICK, John 1849, John Sr. 1766, Margaret 1850
SLIFER, David 1865
SLUSSER, Henry 1809, 1828
SMELTZER, Adam 1769, Leonard 1868, Margaret 1855
SMITH, Adam 1786, Casper 1684, Charles 1695, Christena 1773, Dedrick 1772, Elizabeth 1747, 1748, H. John 1870, Henry 1762, Jacob 1691, 1746, John 1665, 1756, Leonard 1770, Mary 1698, Michael 1719, Nicholas 1657, 1669, Peter 1761, Philip 1722, Rebekah 1683, Richard 1715, 1716, 1721, 1755, Sampson 1823, William 1736, 1817, 1821
SMOUSE, Henry 1777, 1856
SNAVELY, Leonard 1660
SNIDER, Jacob 1685, Jacob Jr. 1794, Sigfrit 1690
SNOUFFER, John 1875, 1877
SNOWNBERGER, Jacob 1678
SNUKE, John 1714, 1730
SNYDER, Mathias 1897
SOMSELL, Devalt 1811
SOWER, John 1707
SOWERS, Balser 1873
SPARROW, Kensey 1673
SPEELMAN, Catharine 1727
SPONSALER, Andrew 1822, Jacob 1795
SPOON, Conrad 1764
SPRIGG, Edward 1640
SPRINGER, Charles 1677
SPROATSMAN, Laws. 1664
STALEY, Henry 1796, 1820, 1835, Jacob 1643, 1644, Joseph 1837, 1840
STALLINGS, Newman 1790, 1827
STALLIONS, Richard 1670
STARR, John 1834, Tabitha 1902
STEEL, Christian 1702
STEINER, Jacob Sr. 1859
STEPHENSON, William 1674
STERLING, Jonathan 1758
STEUART, John 1815, 1819
STEVENS, Jacob 1894
STEVENSON, John 1783, 1792
STEWART, Richard 1676
STICKELL, Sybilla 1774
STICKLE, Valentine 1791
STILLY, Peter 1647, 1814
STIMMEL, Jacob 1836, 1838, Peter 1861
STIMMELL, Jacob 1845, 1851, 1864, Peter 1852, 1858
STITELY, Mary 1705
STOCKTON, Robert 1672
STONE, John Sr. 1884
STONER, Ann 1771, Benedict 1751, Frederick 1656, George 1788, Henry 1682, Isaac 1853, 1793, 1810, Jacob 1797, John Dr. 1780, John Sr. 1781
STONESIFER, John 1785, 1775
STOPPLE, Michael 1718
STORM, Christopher 1880, John 1812, 1839, 1892, Magdalena 1829
STORMS, Isaac 1803, 1816, 1862
STORP, Peter 1668
STORROM, Michael 1708
STOUFFER, Christian 1898, Daniel 1784
STOUP, George 1750
STOVER, Jacob 1693, Philip 1895, 1904
STRAFER, Yocham 1801
STRAILMAN, Henry 1818
STROWS, Nicholas 1807
STRYTE, Godfrey 1692
STUBBY, Robert 1681
STUDAY, Martin 1866
STUDENBAKER, Peter 1637
STUDER, Martin 1805
STULL, Adam 1671, 1743, Christian 1724, 1725, Daniel 1635
STURRUM, Jacob 1700, John 1639, 1645, Michael 1757
SUEMAN, Peter 1717
SUMAN, Peter 1711
SUMMER, John 1867

SWAMLEY, John 1723
SWAN, John 1650
SWEARINGIN, Van 1734
SWEENEY, Edward 1686
SWIGART, Daniel 1889, 1903
TABLER, Melchor 1953, William 1960, 1961
TALBOTT, Elizabeth 1924
TANEY, Michael 1931
TANNEHILL, Carlton 1933
TANNER, Peter 1921
TAWNEY, Adam 1935, Michael 1938
TAYE, Ferdenand 1954
TAYLOR, Joseph 1973, Philpot Chas. 1956
TAYS, Ferdinand 1959
TEDD, Richard 1920
TEMBLE, George 1934
TEMPLIN, Samuel 1975
TENER, Henry 1937
TENNELLY, Thomas 1911, 1914
TETER, Devalt 1917
THOMAS, Amos 1970, 1971, Christian 1927, 1945, Daniel 1916, Gabriel 1942, 1968, 1969, John 1944, 1948, 1957, Notley 1922, Peter 1966, Rebecca 1972, Valentine 1943, William 1941
THOMPSON, Andrew 1947, John 1905, William 1910
THRASHER, Thomas 1962
TICE, Nicholas 1949
TIDY, James 1974
TOBERRY, Joshua 1967
TOBERY, Joshua 1965
TOFLER, Peter 1963
TOMLINSON, Grove 1907, 1908, 1909, Johannah 1919, Nathl. 1912,
TOMS, Henry 1926
TOOLE, James 1950
TOUP, Jacob 1925
TRAIL, Charles 1913
TRESNER, Jacob 1930, 1932
TRINE, Philip 1936, Susannah 1952
TROUT, Jacob 1958, Michael 1940
TROUTMAN, Michael 1939
TROXAL, Peter 1955
TROXALL, Frederick 1946, Peter 1915
TROXEL, Magdalena 1964
TRUCKS, George 1918
TRUNBULL, George 1929
TRUNDLE, John 1923
TUCKER, William 1928
TURNER, John 1951, William 1906

UHLEE, Michael 1979
UMBAUGH, William 1980
UMSTEAD, Nicholas 1978
UNGLEBERRY, Philip 1977
UNSELD, Frederick 1976
VALENTINE, George 1982
VANDIVER, John 1981
VANHORN, Benjamin 1984
VANTREESE, Hartman 1983
VIAN, John 1985
WAGGONER, Adam 2034, Martin 2056
WAGNER, John 2128
WALKER, George 2023, James 2070
WALLACE, Thomas 2035, Williams 2009
WALLARICK, George 1989
WALTER, Daniel 2012, Jacob 2088, 2118, John 2087
WALTZ, Charity 2052, Conrad 2053
WAMPLER, Peter 2073
WANDLE, Jacob 2133
WARD, Robert 1986
WARENFELS, Jacob 2136
WARFIELD, Absalom 2010, 2013, 2018, 2097, 2103, 2111, 2116, Alexander 2125, Charles 2061, Henry 2131, John 2002, 2004
WARMAN, Henry 2095
WARNER, George 2057
WATERS, Azel 2074
WATSON, David 2016
WATT, Robert 2098
WATTS, Charles 2017
WAUGH, Wm. 2011
WEAVER, Daniel 2078, George 2096, John 2006
WEDDLE, Leonard 2104, 2106, Peter 2100, 2101, Susanna 2117
WEINERT, Mathias 2064, Matthias 2066
WELDOR, Saml. Stansby 2005
WELLER, Henry 2044, Jacob 2114, 2135, Philip 2043, 2060
WELTNER, Lodwick 2042
WERENFELTS, Jacob 2099
WERNER, George 2070
WERTENBAKER, Adam 2081, Barbara 2132
WEST, Joseph 2015, 2079, William 1992
WHIP, Martin 2065, Tobias 2073
WHITCRAFT, Marcy 2119, 2120
WHITCROFT, Edward 2077
WHITE, Andrew 2129, 2130, John 1999, Joseph 2091, 2094, Sarah 2134, Philip 2047

WHITENECK, Jno. 2028
WIANT, Yost 2107, 2113
WICKHAM, Nathaniel 2041, Saml. 2027, Samuel 2029, 2030
WIGALE, 2055
WILCOXEN, Roger 1990
WILDS, John 2007
WILE, George 2085
WILLETT, Edward 2020, Thomas 1998
WILLIAMS, John 2008, William 2000, 2019, 2021,
WILLIAR, John Sr. 2115
WILLIARD, Devalt 2105
WILLIS, Henry 2127
WILLSON, John 2031, William 2024, 2062, 2068
WILSON, Absolam 1993, 1995, Christr. 2026, John 2001, Priscilla 1996, 1997
WINDSOR, Notley Benj. 1988
WINE, Frederick 2046
WINEGARDNER, Abraham 2092, 2093
WINEMILLER, Henry 2109, 2110
WINHOLTS, Frederick 2037
WINHOLTZ, Conrad 2051, Frederick 2058
WINPEAGLER, George 2063
WINTZ, George 2059
WIRTZ, Jacob 2014
WISE, Francis 1991, George 2032, Joseph 2123, 2126,
WISINGER, Lodowick 2033
WISSINGER, Catharine 2072
WITHROW, William 2049
WITMORE, Abraham 2124, Michael 2086
WOLF, Adam 2048, John 2025, Valentine 2039
WOLFE, Henry 2090
WOLVERTON, Isaac 2054
WOOD, Catharine 2071, Henry 2075, Jacob 1987, John 2076, Joseph 2038, 2067
WOODRING, Philip 2089
WOOLFE, Christopher 2082
WOOLHATER, George 2003
WOOLSEY, George 2045
WOOLSLAGER, Nicholas 2069
WORMAN, Andrew 2112, 2121, 2122, Jacob 2084, Mary 2102, 2108,
WORTHINGTON, Charles 2036
WRIGHT, John 2040, Joseph 2022
WYVEL, William 1994
YANTIS, Daniel 2150, 2153, Jacob 2159, John 2158
YENGLEN, John 2139
YERGER, Henry 2145
YINGLING, Margaret 2149
YOHAM, Michael 2137
YON, Yoham 2138
YONTZ, Catharine 2143, George 2142
YOST, Harmon John 2146, Harmon Jno. 2148, John 2154, 2155, 2160, Lodwick 2144, Ludwick 2147
YOUNG, Hezekiah 2156, 2157, Jacob 2151, 2152, John Engle 2140, 2141
ZACHARIAS, Daniel 2161
ZADOCK, Frances 2162
ZERECH, Antony 2163
ZIMMERMAN, Benjamin 2165, 2166, George 2164, 2167
ZOLMAN, Adam 2168

www.ingramcontent.com/pod-product-compliance
Lightning Source LLC
Chambersburg PA
CBHW071759040426
42446CB00012B/2621